An UnCommon LIFE

Surviving The Loss Of A Gifted Child

Merry Rosenfield

AN UNCOMMON LIFE
Surviving the Loss of a Gifted Child
Copyright © Merry Rosenfield, 2010

This book may be ordered online at:
www.merryrosenfield.com
orders@merryrosenfield.com

For more information on Cedar
www.cedarbennett.org

This is a work of nonfiction. All of the characters, names, incidents, organizations and dialogue in this autobiography are or were part of the author's life. To protect their identities, the author has changed the names and altered the appearances of some of the people who are in this book.

ISBN-13: 978-0-9844523-4-7 | ISBN-10: 0-9844523-4-6
Library of Congress Control: 2010902566

THE MAGIC ZOO INC.
P.O. Box 1116 Clearwater, FL 33757

Edited by Kate Kitchen
Cover Photograph by Wayne Porter
All Illustrations by Cedar Bennett Rosenfield
Cover Design & Layout by Eli Blyden | CrunchTimeGraphics.net

Printed in the United States of America

MEMOIR

For two young artists I love –
Sam and Ada

About the Author

Merry Rosenfield began writing as a child, after falling in love with the simple beauty of Japanese haiku poetry.

As a young parent, she wrote poetry and created stories for her family to enjoy, believing that art should be a part of everyday life.

Today Merry designs animal-themed jewelry and runs her company, *The Magic Zoo*, with her husband Ed. Happily, her son, daughter-in-law and two of her three grandchildren live just blocks away, making it easy for her to continue sharing her stories.

An Uncommon Life is her first published book.

Photo by: Richel Lavette

About the Illustrations

Occasionally I'd hear Cedar laughing to herself in the next room.

"What's so funny?"

"Come see what I just drew!" I'd put down my work to check out the creation she was so tickled about. It might be a sketch of a funny looking man with a goofy hat and big stomach, or a quick line drawing of a sultry movie star from the 1920s. Sometimes she would spend half a day designing pen and ink deco-looking posters in honor of the actors and actresses that she loved—the men and women who starred in movies and plays from the first part of the 20th century.

It was Eli, our layout artist who brilliantly suggested incorporating Cedar's artwork into my book.

My husband and I searched through the sketch books and portfolios she had left behind, looking for drawings to head each chapter. For some, we lucked out and found a perfect image, like the pen and ink zebra I used for Chapter Seven. But mostly the drawings we chose were dependent on our own sense of creative relevancy.

It reminded me of a game Cedar and I played years ago. I would fold a piece of paper in four sections. Cedar started off by sketching an imaginative head on the top section, and with her drawing folded over so I couldn't see what she had created, I would add a neck and torso. Then it was her turn to draw the waist and hips (again, folding the paper first to make the torso invisible to her) and finally, blind to her last effort, I'd finish with the legs and feet. When unfolded, the resulting hodgepodge of male and female, fat and skinny, hobo and sophisticate sent us into uncontrolled spasms of laughter.

So I'm sure Cedar would have been amused by our dilemma of trying to match her unrelated artwork to my writing. But I also think she would have loved the idea of another collaborative effort with her mom.

Photo by: Terry Belden

Acknowledgments

This memoir grew from one and a half years of early morning typing while gazing at the oak and mango trees in my backyard, quietly remembering. How to communicate a life within a few hundred pages? It wasn't an easy task, and I often found myself weeping with the joys and sorrows of those memory's shadows.

I wish to thank my husband Ed Rosenfield for his quiet enthusiasm, much needed hugs and unshakable belief that I could, and would complete this book, our family's story. I wish every wife had a spouse so thoughtful, loving and dear.

I want to thank my daughter-in-law Diana Rosenfield for her encouragement and for spotting the grammatical details that slipped my notice early on. Diana has become a second daughter to me, and I know that she and Cedar would have been great pals.

A special thank you to Diana's mother, Nancy Forrest, an old and dear friend. Nancy read my manuscript and spotted things even her attentive daughter had missed.

Wayne Porter photographed the cover of this book. Thank you, Wayne, for capturing Cedar's beauty and grace so perfectly with your camera.

My editor, Kate Kitchen, became a friend during the process of her work. Thank you for your encouragement, your sensitivity and your spot-on editing.

To my cover artist and layout man, Eli Blyden—my grateful thanks for your ability to take my words, Cedar's art and Wayne's photograph and create a whole that communicates so well.

And to all the friends and family mentioned within these pages; thank you for enriching Cedar's life.

TABLE OF CONTENTS

1

THE MANGO TREE

In the spring after our daughter Cedar died, we planted fruit trees in our Florida backyard.

Under a sprawling little fig we placed a carved garden angel with wings folded over her back like a resting butterfly. We didn't picture Cedar as an angel, but there was something spiritual and playful about the small statue that reminded us of her.

Twenty years earlier, when Cedar was just six months old, she played on a quilt beneath our fig tree in California. I have an old photo of her squinting into the camera—sitting fat, naked and perfectly straight-backed beside the gnarled grey trunk. In late summer this fig produced bushels of delicious black fruit, which we picked warm and slightly soft right from the tree. The inside was ruby red and made a satisfying crunch with each bite, like a Fig Newton come to life.

But our Florida tree didn't fare so well. Long before its first autumn, all the leaves were gone and by the following spring we had to admit it had mysteriously perished. We dug it up and planted another one. "We'll put this one right next to the house," Ed said, thinking the new location would discourage root-hungry nematodes. The little angel was nestled beneath it.

This fig clung to life through a blistering subtropical summer. Despite tender feedings and twice weekly watering, its thin branches were black and crisp by August.

But one of the mango trees we planted that first sad spring grew to nearly 15 feet, and after three years produced a single delectable fruit. I picked it rosy and fragrant, keeping it on the kitchen counter for two more days before eating it.

We placed the now homeless angel beneath a graceful mango branch. This seemed appropriate because Cedar loved a good ripe mango. She would peel a whole one over the kitchen sink, knifing off the juicy, yellow-orange pulp into a bowl, then gnawing off what stuck to the flat seed in the middle.

A lot of those very seeds sprouted in the compost heap, one of which we transplanted into a more suitable spot where it has shot up to ten gangly, flowerless feet. I have asked Ed to chop it down and let the other two mangos have the sun and soil energy it's taking up, but I don't think he has the heart.

2

THE ARRIVAL

After losing Cedar, even my earliest memories of her intensified. I watched them tenderly, grateful for this precious mental film.

October 4, 1981 was the day Cedar was born. I was laboring in the huge back seat of our black and red Chevy Impala, lying down and shifting from one side to the other as if there really were a way to be more comfortable. We were driving David to the baby sitter's at eleven in the morning, en route to the hospital.

The night before, I had eaten too much strawberry shortcake. It was delicious at the time, but a terrible thing to be full on during that sleepless night of early labor. As we drove, our four-year-old son's dark eyes stared back at me, wide with alarm. At all the red lights, Ed twisted in his seat to smile at me. "Look how strong Mommy is," he said to David, reassuring them both.

We pulled into the driveway by Bob and Nancy's apartment in Hollywood. Bob loped down the concrete stairs and sauntered across the driveway to the car. "David, are you ready?" His kind blue eyes twinkled above a magnificent Roman nose.

"I guess." David swiveled towards me from the front seat, brow furrowed. "Mommy, what will I do? Diana's too little to play with for all that time."

Diana was Bob and Nancy's two-year-old daughter. "Well, maybe we won't be too long. As soon as your little brother or sister is here, Daddy will let you know."

"Okay, don't forget!" He dashed from the front seat and grabbed Bob's hand, waving us off with a serious face.

Ed and I headed down Sunset Boulevard, palm trees and high rises outlined softly against the white L.A. morning.

David's birth had resulted in an emergency C-section, but we'd searched all over L.A. and found Dr. R. from Israel who didn't believe in repeating Cesareans unless it was absolutely necessary to save a life.

He practiced at Cedars-Sinai Medical Center in Beverly Hills. That's where Hollywood's movie stars go to have their babies, or treatment for drug overdoses or whatever else comes up in the human side of their glamorous lives. Not that we were wealthy, far from it. We lived in a tiny rental house in Glendale with the black fig tree in the back and a lemon tree so prolific I sold the fruit to the owner of the produce stand down the street for extra cash.

We arrived at the main lobby where an aide put me in a wheelchair at the curb and took me inside. Ed parked the car. When the admitting nurse asked me how far apart my pains were, I realized, startled, that I'd felt nothing since we arrived. "Well they *were* about twenty minutes apart." I shook my head, puzzled.

The nurse said, "Honey, that's not unusual. We're going to take you down to a labor room, and you just relax. Dr. R. will be here in no time." She was young and pretty, tight black curls framing her flawless chocolate skin. Ed had returned and followed our little procession down the hall toward the maternity wing.

The room was freezing. I changed into the open-backed hospital gown. The nurse said, "Step up on the stool and have a seat, Sweetheart." I'm sure she was at least five years younger than me and must have weighed about a hundred and ten to my pregnant one-sixty.

I hoisted my bulk gracelessly onto the papered cot.

Five minutes before the doctor arrived, my contractions were back— tight, urgent cramps streaming forward in waves. "I guess I'm having a baby," I said turning my face toward Ed with a watery smile. He kissed my forehead.

Dr. R. stepped into the room, exhausted from an all-night birth and having had only three hours sleep since. He was a short, neat man who smelled mildly of antiseptic soap and spoke with an Israeli accent. "Well, let's see how we're doing here." He examined me, smiled at Ed and said to him conspiratorially, "We could never do what they do." I felt a flush of pride.

I held Ed's hand and breathed slowly through each contraction, my eyes widening at the crest. "Maybe I should've practiced more," I told Ed.

"Nah, you're doing great," he smiled.

Then transition arrived. Now the contractions were too long, a continuous tsunami of agonizing discomfort. After the second one, I was lost and screamed through it, embarrassed in the seconds remaining before the next wave hit. By the third one, I was desperately out of control and even Ed had tears streaming down his face. Dr. R. looked at me sharply.

"Merry, what's happening? Are you feeling intense pain anywhere?" He seemed a little panicked, obviously worried about uterine rupture. I was sorry to cause trouble and apologized helplessly.

"No, that's not it; I'm just having a terrible time." I was dreading the next wave, trying to prepare myself.

"I can't give you anything because we would have no way of knowing if something *did* go wrong," he explained carefully.

I was wheeled to the delivery room, but I have no memory of that. The contractions had mercifully altered and I was grunting and pushing, in the throes of that other and completely different primal urge. Ed said "Watch the mirror, you can see the top of the baby's head!" but that was something I couldn't do. I kept my eyes tightly shut—concentrating, straining.

My final push sent the baby from crowded warmth to fathomless cold—indignantly, with a howl of despairing protest. Dr. R. announced, "A girl!" Ed and I both wept. The nurse wrapped our baby in a heated blanket and put her on my chest where I kissed her still-wet head. For over seven months David had assured me I was carrying his sister, but now in my arms, this baby girl seemed an improbable miracle.

They wheeled me somewhere else and brought us a delectable dinner—roasted chicken with vegetables on real china with cloth napkins.

"How are you doing?" Ed asked.

"I'm exhausted. And hoarse from screaming."

Our baby arrived in the arms of a large, smiling nurse. "She's a hungry one!" she said, and handed her to me. "Do you need some help?"

"No, I nursed my son for two years," I said with a smile.

But I wasn't prepared for her first mighty suckle. "Wow, I've forgotten what that was like!" I was grimacing and breathing hard.

Ed rubbed my neck and kissed my cheek. "She's so beautiful."

We spent the night in a private room where Ed was provided with a bed so he could stay with me. Cedar lay beneath a brilliant Van Gogh print in a plastic bassinet near the door, making delicate newborn chirping sounds. "Listen," Ed smiled, his head cocked so he could hear her better. "Maybe she'll be a singer like her mama."

3

GRANDMA KATE

B ack home, Cedar slept in a crib at the foot of our bed. She woke me up several times a night to nurse, but I didn't mind. I held her in my arms, rocking and peaceful, still basking in the glow of her arrival. I was enjoying this second bout of new motherhood without having to heal from simultaneous major surgery.

When Cedar was two months old, I put her in a yellow and brown-striped umbrella stroller, preparing to jog around our neighborhood before David and Ed woke up.

"Let's see that beautiful baby!" Don from the Jiffy Lube on the corner lot next to our house strode across the blacktop drive separating us. He bent down for a closer look, holding his greasy hands behind his back. As my pregnancy had progressed, he had taken friendly interest and even waved us off to the hospital when it was time. "What's her name?"

"Cedar," I told him.

"Did you name her after the hospital?" he laughed.

"No, we just liked the name." I smiled at him.

She cooed quietly as we jogged past stately old homes on some streets and small bungalows with Hispanic children playing in the yard on others. The morning was cool and the sky white, sunlight struggling to peer through the thick layer of smog.

Grandma Vera and my mom Grandma Kate had separately sent their first granddaughter similar pink outfits in a tiny rosebud pattern. I dressed her in one of them and asked David to hold her while I snapped a photo. "Wait while I get my hat!" David searched for the battered throwaway his dad had given him the day before. "There, now I'm ready!" He held his sister carefully around the waist, gently kissing the back of her head.

When Cedar was five months old, she laughed for the first time. David was in the back seat of our Chevy while I held the wiggly Cedar in front. We were waiting for Ed to pick up dinner at the neighborhood Safeway.

"What's Dad getting us?" David popped up over the seat behind us, surprising his sister. Cedar smiled at her brother then giggled–a brand new sound like a fledgling's first bubbly warble.

David and I laughed, and I congratulated him. "Mr. Bear, that's the first time she's laughed! She thinks you're funny!"

David couldn't get her to repeat it when Ed got back to the car, so the next day he decided to put on a show for her, something he was positive would make *him* laugh.

David hid behind the drapes. Ed and I sat with Cedar on the brown-striped daybed opposite his impromptu stage. Cedar smiled and watched carefully, tense and thrilled by something she knew was about to happen. Suddenly David's Teddy Bear flew into the room from behind the curtains. It was propelled by an invisible force and accompanied by David's high pitched, "Whoop!" Cedar dissolved in baby giggles and collapsed on her right side and into my arms.

For weeks afterwards, she looked at her brother expectantly, waiting for him to do something amusing. In fact, he was the only one who could make her laugh for the longest time.

A month later Grandma Kate flew from Cincinnati to visit. We headed up the airport escalator to meet her but she was obliviously riding the one next to us on her way down to baggage claim.

"Mom!" I shouted. She turned her head, saw Cedar in my arms and burst into tears. "Stay at the bottom, we'll be right there!"

I handed Cedar to Ed, took David's hand and rushed down the escalator to her. With Mom, I never quite knew what she would do so I hoped she'd stay put. She did, waiting where I told her to, a big smile on her trembling red lips. "Merry!" We hugged and both of us wept. She hadn't seen me in over five years, and now I had two children. It must have been overwhelming.

Mom chatted to David in the back seat all the way home. Our son was fascinated with his grandmother. She didn't look or sound like other people. Mom was 5 feet tall with short curly grey hair, wide-set hazel eyes and prominent, high cheekbones—a gift from Native American ancestry. Her lips were full, and almost always painted bright red. She spoke with a soft Kentucky drawl, inexplicably unfaded after forty years of living in Ohio. Mom was opinionated, outspoken and laughed and cried with equal ease.

And she loved babies. As soon as we got out of the car, she grabbed Cedar, who looked a little perplexed but didn't protest. "Look at dose wittle brown arms. Just like wolls from de oven!" She was prodding the fat on Cedar's forearm and speaking baby talk in a dialect Cedar was unfamiliar with. She watched her grandmother carefully.

Mom was a professional artist, and prying her from her freelance illustration work across the country was no small feat, even to visit her first granddaughter. "I actually got her here!" I whispered to Ed that night, still amazed.

The second evening of her visit, the five of us sat at the dining room table where I served lobster tail for the first and only time. "This is delicious!" she said and I pretended it was no big deal.

Mom showered David with gifts, his favorite being the brightly-colored Smurf-printed sheets she bought at the local mall. "They're so loud I doubt you'll be able to sleep tonight," she said to her puzzled grandson.

When it was time to go, Mom kissed us all on the lips, down-home southern style.

"We'll see you at Holly's next spring," I told her as we waved our final goodbyes. My sister was planning a reunion at her Chicago home the following year.

Later that spring Cedar started to crawl, and I took her to the backyard where she headed straight toward my vegetable patch, bare butt covered in mud. I let her play naked on an old green quilt under the fig tree, but now she could leave its confines and I followed her around the yard while David laughed.

"Mom, what's she doing?" he asked just as I'd looked away for one second. Cedar was eyeing a fistful of dirt and grass, guiding it carefully toward her open mouth.

"No baby girl, that's not for eating." She squalled while I brushed out her hand. "C'mon, let's take a bath." She bobbed her entire body "yes," squealing delightedly as I carried her into the house.

Cedar walked at ten months, taking her first wobbly step while Ed was at work. He sold framed nature photographs door to door in business offices in the Valley and as far south as Newport Beach. This is what I did, too, before I had gotten too big with Cedar. I tried it once after she was born, wearing her on my chest in a green corduroy snuggly, holding David's hand and dragging a box of photos on a luggage cart. I walked down Brand Avenue in Glendale, in and out of car dealerships. "I came by to show you some framed photographs," I said, bouncing my awakening newborn while David announced, "I need to pee" in the first glass showroom we had entered. I think I embarrassed the lead salesman.

"No, I'm sorry we don't allow soliciting here," he told me hurriedly. In the second dealership, the receptionist was patronizing, in the third kindly but uninterested, in the fourth, annoyed with the world and our little entourage specifically. I walked the six blocks home, hot with humiliation. I'd failed to make a red cent toward our survival. Ed understood. He had thought it was a bad idea to begin with. "Just be a mommy," he hugged me.

David took big brothering seriously. He taught Cedar how to sit on his hot wheels, where she held onto the plastic bars and grinned, feet too far from the pedals. But she was content to watch *him* zoom down the sidewalk from the vantage point of her stroller, eyes glowing with appreciation. "Hurry up, Mom!" David shouted from a block away, making sure I noticed how fast and far he had gone.

We took walks every few days to the Public Library, where David always checked out fifteen books; that was a number I could remember so I could count them and make sure they all got returned on time. I read daily to both kids, Cedar's eyes open as she nursed and David next to us, short legs straight across the width of the couch. *Little Bear's Visit* was one of my favorites, although I couldn't read the part when his mother let her pet robin go free without a little quiver of grief in my voice. "What's wrong, Mommy?" David asked the first time this happened.

"I always get sad when she knows it's time to let the bird go free."

"It's Okay," he said, patting my hand.

4

GRANDMA VERA

When Cedar was two and David was six, we moved to Florida from California, traveling three thousand miles in an old aqua and white laundry-step van. We were driving to Clearwater, where The Church of Scientology's major center had relocated a few years earlier. We had both been taking classes at a Scientology organization in Hollywood, but Ed and I were tired of smog and freeways and thought the environment might be a little slower paced in Florida. Along the way, David asked "Can we go swimming at the beach?" Our trips to the Pacific had involved a little wading, but even then our teeth chattered. The stories we'd heard of bathtub temperature Gulf waters were enticing, and ended up being entirely true.

After the first day traveling, Ed and I were hoarse from shouting past the unmuffled engine noise. "I guess the delivery guys didn't worry much about conversation!" I yelled.

"What?"

"Never mind." Our seats creaked on ancient springs even on the smoothest of roads, and pitched crazily on tubular steel stems when we hit a pothole or rough patch.

We set up Cedar's wooden crib behind the passenger seat and David's bed on the other side. The kids poked at my head through the metal cage behind my seat. "I know you're there!" I shouted back, inviting giggles. Strictly speaking, our traveling arrangements weren't perfect—no child seat and nowhere to fasten one securely, anyway.

Instead of over-nighting in motels, we camped in the National Forest or parked at rest stops. Ed and I slept in a platform bed in the very back, our meager luggage piled underneath.

While we rode across the Arizona desert, David Grisman crooned, *Old and in the Way* from our portable tape player. I spooned bites of canned cheese ravioli into the kids' mouths while the sun sat on the horizon, morphing the desert from parched dreamscape to plains of multi-layered crimson and shadow.

Ed was the only one who had been to Florida, back when he belonged to a Jewish fraternity at Washington University and had traveled with the boys to Ft. Lauderdale on spring break. I pumped him for details but he replied "All I can remember are white sand beaches and girls in bikinis."

From Georgia on, the air got heavier and wetter until we arrived in Florida where our first afternoon crashed in with a thunderstorm. We parked off the freeway, three of us enraptured by an hour of bone-jarring thunder and jagged swaths of evil looking lightening cutting across the blue-black sky. "Mommy, I'm scared!' Cedar was curled up on my lap, afraid to look.

I thought Clearwater was exotic. Slim anole lizards dashed in front of my feet on neighborhood sidewalks, fragrant orange and grapefruit trees bloomed in people's yards, lush greenery and hibiscus flowers seemed to be everywhere.

We rented a little blue house on Tuskawilla Drive from someone we knew. It was in a working class neighborhood with dozens of children David's age. The next door neighbor kid was named Freddie and his dad was in prison. This little boy was one to keep an eye on, I remember thinking then, but now I can't remember what he did that worried me.

A few months later we moved into a dilapidated house a couple of streets over. The landlord had just kicked out his previous renters, a crowd of beer-swigging bikers who had nudged the place further toward the edge of compost. He offered us free rent for three months if we would clean up the broken glass and beer tabs in the yard and the piles of garbage inside, and very cheap rent after that. It had no air conditioning and so many gaps in the walls and floors that inch-long palmetto bugs could visit when they pleased. They sneaked up the walls at night and sometimes, to my horror, buzzed lazily across the room like miniature helicopters. But the house sat on a big piece of land with a giant oak in the back corner of the lot and was in a quiet neighborhood.

Cedar adored her big brother and followed him around wherever he went. She had fine blond hair that hung in a permanent fringe in front of her eyes, and when she was a teenager, she told me all her memories of that time were through a blond haze.

One summer afternoon David rushed inside with his sister and two neighborhood boys.

"Tommy, Freddie and me want to pull Cedar up in the oak tree. We have a pulley and it'll be safe, I promise!" I looked at their earnest faces dying for me to say yes.

"Please, Mommy!" Cedar begged when she noticed the left side of my mouth drawn sideways in characteristic and questioning suspicion.

David dragged me outside toward the tree. "Come on Mom, I'll show you!" A fat frayed rope hung on one side of the pulley, an ancient device I had never noticed, mounted on a thick branch halfway up the tree, about twenty feet in the air. There was a crate on the ground, attached to the other side of the rope, Cedar's lift. She ran over and sat down in it with a sandy plop.

"Now pull me up!" she commanded.

"Sweetie, I'm sorry but it just isn't safe. If the rope broke halfway up you could be hurt," I was trying to be diplomatic.

"Mom, I promise not to hurt her. Come on, just one time?" he looked at me, heartbroken.

"No honey, we can't do this. I don't really want you boys playing with this. I'm sorry. I know it sounds like fun, but we can't risk it."

He looked at the ground and mumbled, "Oh, all right," but Cedar was furious with me.

"Mommy, I *want* to go up!"

"I know, but why don't we bake cookies instead?"

"What kind?"

"How about carob chip?"

"Hurray!" The pulley was forgotten, but Ed dismantled it just to be on the safe side.

Ed was going to school fulltime, studying to be a Scientology counselor. I studied there too, part time, and also found a job making polymer clay animal jewelry for a local designer. She sold them to big stores like Macy's and little boutiques all over the country—and even Hawaii, where she'd lived for a while. I spent hours on my first project from her, which was not an animal at all but a tray of calla lily pins, mostly white.

They ended up ruined, covered in fine dust from what I imagined to be a protected spot on top of the refrigerator where I'd set them after my day's work. I called her apologetically the next day. Karen said "Look, the way to keep your unfinished jewelry clean is just put a piece of white paper on top till you're ready to bake them."

She sounded resigned, but I was mortified. "I'm so sorry," I told her, but she insisted on paying me anyway for the time I'd worked.

"You're still apprenticing," she said.

The night of that humbling experience we heard something scrabbling around in the attic right above our bed. What in the world could *that* be? It went on for most of a sleepless eight hours and the next morning I called an exterminator.

"You have rats," he said bluntly after crawling around up there for fifteen minutes. Actually he called them fruit rats which I'm sure was just a euphemism. He recommended poisoning them. "Don't worry, I'll put the bait in your attic," It still seemed creepy, but having rats was far worse.

"Maybe we should get a cat," Ed suggested later. The bait was already in place, but a cat might be a good deterrent for any future rodent squatters.

I thought David and Cedar should have a pet anyway, now that we were settled for a while. "How soon can we get one?" they wanted to know when I mentioned it over tuna casserole that evening.

The next weekend we made a trip to the local SPCA shelter to look over the inmates. "Aww, look at this *kitten!*" the kids were standing dewy-eyed in front of a cage, poking their fingers inside the bars to reach a little ball of grey fluff. He mewed at them, eyes round with wonder.

"Sweeties, we need to get a full grown cat, so he can keep the rats away," I reasoned.

"But mom," David started to say.

Then he noticed the tabby cat watching us from across the room. She was rubbing against the bars, purring and blinking her big green-gold eyes fetchingly. "Look how pretty!" Cedar was transfixed.

"May we take her from the cage?" I asked the volunteer.

"Of course."

I picked her up and she held onto me in her version of a cat hug, her arms on my shoulders like a child's. "Look how sweet she is!" I exclaimed. I read her bio. "One-year-old neutered female, doesn't get along well with other cats and not tolerant of children." That seemed odd. She seemed so affectionate.

Cedar gave her a gentle pat. "Let's name her Tiger," she said.

"We'll see. Do you really think this cat is the one? Ed, read this." He looked at the report.

"She seems friendly enough. Kids, what do you think?"

"I love her!" Cedar said passionately.

"I think she picked us," David cocked his head so he could look into her eyes. "Didn't you?' he asked her while giving her a scratch on the neck.

She came home with us in a box, mewing and howling the entire two miles. When I opened up the box in our living room, she popped out like a toy on springs. Cedar laughed. "What do *you* think we should name her, Mommy?" she asked.

"How about Molly?" I suggested. "Molly." Cedar tried it out. "Yes, that will be her name."

Cedar adored her. They slept together from that first night. She wasn't yet three years old, but she was gentle with Molly, and it was a good thing because this cat definitely would take no guff.

We didn't have a cat door in the house, but a hole in the floor in the same room where I made my jewelry, just big enough for a slim female cat to exit. It made Ed and me laugh. The entire house was a joke, such a far cry from the middle class homes we had grown up in. I secretly gave thanks that my mom wasn't much of a traveler.

We weren't so lucky with Grandma Vera, who surprised us by inviting herself for a visit at the same time Ed's sister and husband would be staying with us. Vera had always been stubborn, but old age had intensified this and turning her tactfully from this plan proved impossible. "Of course we'd love to have you, but we don't have an extra bedroom." I couldn't envision my proper, perfectly groomed mother-in-law stepping one foot inside this house.

"That's fine; I can stay at a motel near by," she told me. It was hopeless.

"Ed, what'll we do?"

"Don't worry about it. Susan and Larry will get here the day before, which should help." Naively, Ed believed Vera was resigned to our eccentricities.

I cleaned the entire house, scouring bathroom tiles and scrubbing all the floors on my hands and knees. I even painted David and Cedar's bedroom a cheerful sky blue and sewed festive animal print curtains for their windows. But the living room she would see as soon as she stepped inside had gloomy wood paneling from the 60s, and a termite-ridden grey floor full of cracks. My *studio* was a salvaged folding table propped up against one wall. And there was that hole in the floor for the cat. I couldn't do much about that, but it was in a dark corner that I hoped she wouldn't notice.

She arrived around noon on a Thursday in June. "Hello, Vera." We pecked each other's cheeks and hugged delicately. I was still the gentile girl she'd rather not have in the family, but she had stopped complaining about me once we had our second child. Ed had a hard time believing me when I said "Your mom told me she was sorry you didn't marry a Jewish girl." But that had been seven years ago, when David was still a baby.

I tried a whimsical approach. "Welcome to our little cabin."

"I see," she looked around unsmiling, small dark eyes taking in every detail with still perfect vision. Thankfully, it was too early in the day for palmetto bugs.

"Grandma Vera!" David and Cedar ran to her, hugging her clumsily around the hips.

"Hey, let Grandma sit down!" I wasn't sure of her steadiness so I brushed the kids gently from her skirt. She looked noticeably frailer than her visit to California three years earlier. She perched gingerly on the edge of our shabby yellow couch, reaching in her bag for the children's books she had brought from Kansas City.

Susan and Larry's footsteps clumped hollowly on the wooden front porch. They were back early from an afternoon soak in the Gulf, thank goodness. "Vera's here," I stepped outside and smiled at Susan, gazing toward the heavens meaningfully. She was holding Jesse, rosy cheeked and festooned with the inevitable curls he had inherited from both his parents. Larry congenially hauled bags of diapers and other baby paraphernalia in quilted cloth bags as he stooped through the door. He had three grown children from his first marriage, and a whole new crop starting with this chubby five-month-old.

Larry wasn't Jewish either, but I think Vera accepted him more easily. Besides being a home owner he was a minor celebrity, having published dozens of children's science related books. He was *somebody* in her eyes.

Susan held Jesse on her hip. "Don't get up mom," She bent and hugged her mother with her left arm.

"Oh Jesse," Vera reached for him with trembling arms, and Susan plopped him in her lap.

I have a photograph of that exact moment. Vera is sitting in our disturbingly dark living room with her plump, ivory-skinned grandson held close in her arms. David and Cedar are on either side of them, brown as berries from the Florida sun and grinning happily. Vera's either *purposely* unsmiling or caught in the exact wrong millisecond.

The visit, which only lasted a few more days, was at least civil. The weather in Kansas City, a relative who recently had gall bladder surgery, and which local restaurant served the best grouper sandwich were safe topics, discussed at length. The adults may have been bored, but David and Cedar were electrified by her visit. They walked Grandma around the block, pointing out lizards and the cotton plant that grew in one neighbor's yard. "Did you know that alligators live here?" David asked her, wide-eyed.

"Really?" Vera said, her eyes twinkling. She thought he was teasing.

"Yes. We just saw one at the pond last week," he told her truthfully.

"You'd better be careful," she laughed.

At dinner that night David asked, "What was my Daddy like when he was little?" She told them the story of how once little Eddie ran away from her with a wet diaper on, shouting "I'm *dwy*!" They giggled, imagining their father in miniature.

This was Vera's last trip to see her grandchildren. She died the next year from pneumonia after landing in the hospital with a hip fracture delivered by a careless driver's bump on one rainy Missouri night. I ended up grateful for whatever prescient stubbornness had ensured that final summer's visit.

5

ʃMALL ARTIʃTʃ

My work produced a lot of extra scraps that I couldn't seem to turn into the angular abstract earrings Karen wanted me to make from them. When I tried, the shapes were always too round or irregular or funny looking in some other way. When she gave up on me, I gave the scraps to David and Cedar.

They became tiny snakes, snowmen, and Christmas wreaths, which put them to much better use; I still have those. If I'd made earrings they would have been tossed out long ago by customers tired of their 1980s accessories.

One of my favorites is a colorful parrot, about three inches long with all sorts of surprising details like little strands of purple clay suspended from an orange head and a body shaped vaguely like a fish. Cedar's tiny four-year-old fingerprints are the best part of this for me. Every place she pushed to make the shape is a little indentation of her intention, and under a bright light with my glasses on I can see miniature swirls from her thumb and index finger.

I keep this one carefully wrapped in tissue paper in the old popcorn tin with my other Christmas ornaments, but it's pretty durable. That clay parrot will still be around when I'm long gone.

I also have a little round snowman made from three smooshed together white clay balls. This one has a delicately detailed carrot nose, little black button eyes and teensy coal mouth with a green muffler thrown back over one snowy shoulder. David sat opposite Cedar designing this one at the kitchen table, his tongue compressed between his lips and his eyes squinting in concentration.

I taught the kids my favorite childhood game, "Make Something, Make Something Out of It." It started with a scribble on a piece of paper, passed to a sibling responsible for turning it into something recognizable, if fantastic. Monsters, animals, trees and buildings were birthed from one carelessly drawn line. There were no strict rules. You could turn the scribble upside down or sideways to get inspiration.

"That's too hard!" Cedar complained. David had just drawn a tricky one, full of surprising wiggles.

"Here, just turn it like this," I angled the scribble and Cedar laughed.

"I know what it looks like now!" She covered her drawing with her cupped hand. "Here, a turtle!" she shouted, shoving the drawing towards her brother victoriously.

A year earlier David had seen the Popeye movie with Robin Williams and Shelly Duvall and still sang *I'm Popeye the Sailor Man* with a corncob pipe worn rakishly on the side of his mouth, one eye *squinched* up for effect like the cartoon character. David was a performer at heart, even at age seven. I have a recording of him singing, *I've been Working on the Railroad.* When he got to the part "Someone's in the kitchen with Dinah, someone's in the kitchen I know-oh-oh-oh. Someone's in the kitchen with Dinah, strumming on the old BAM-BO", he raised his voice in a crescendo, emphasizing the non-word that I didn't have the heart to correct.

We didn't have a TV. If the kids were bored they sang, made up skits or drew pictures. On cool mornings the three of us pedaled through our sleepy neighborhood streets on the perfectly good bikes we had picked up at Goodwill.

On the back of mine Ed attached a yellow child seat which Cedar rode in happily, pretending (as she told me years later) that I was her chauffeur.

6

MILL VALLEY

We had lived in Florida for two years. Ed had completed his training as a counselor and I had learned how to supervise classes for people new to Scientology. We decided to move back to California, joining the staff at a mission of our church in San Francisco. We were full of youthful exuberance and a fresh purpose to help.

In the spring of 1986 we traveled west in the same laundry van, but now there was a litter box in the driver's step. Molly was a surprisingly patient traveler in her youth (she was just a few years old) and she drank water from a bowl held to her while she sat on my lap so it wouldn't spill. But she spent most of the journey hiding behind the wall of clothes that hung in the middle of the van, at the foot of our platform bed.

We rented a home in Oakland that came with three chickens and a rooster in the backyard. David named one of them Grand High Witch after a character in a Roald Dahl book. When David searched for the eggs she laid in our overgrown back yard she chased him, pecking him in the butt. The other two chickens were more demure, Henrietta and Little Red Hen.

The rooster woke us at five-thirty a.m. and after a week, we complained to our landlord who took him away and let him loose in China town. We never discussed this with the kids.

Ed and I wanted to move to Marin County, across the Golden Gate Bridge and under the painted rainbow arch. Then we could drive to work instead of taking the BART, and we'd be just a short way from Mt. Tamalpais and the beach.

Eventually we did rent a tiny house in Mill Valley. It perched on a hill just up from Sweetwater's, a club with live music you could listen to from the front porch on Friday and Saturday nights.

Our street was called Madrona. Our part of it was a series of stone steps that started at the bottom of the hill where everybody parked, and led to little houses on either side all the way up to another road at the very top. From the street level at the bottom you could see the old brick library on the left that appeared in *Invasion of the Body Snatchers*, filmed in Mill Valley in 1956. A quiet man named Dale lived just opposite it in a wood and glass house behind a wall of bamboo that he had planted years earlier.

Ours was the next house, a few steps from the stone walkway on the left, behind the library and with a front yard full of seven-foot-high anise plants that grew there happily and unmolested. The house was made of wood, probably someone's vacation place in the 1920s.

The door off the front porch opened to a tiny living room with red flower print wall paper and a floor to ceiling wall heater where we stood to get warm on foggy days.

The kitchen could have been in a farmhouse; there was a round white table in the middle of the linoleum floor and a deep enamel sink with a window above it that faced our next door neighbor's house. A couple of friendly musicians named Roberta and Bob lived there, just a few yards away. At night we could hear them practice as soft electric sounds from Bob's keyboard drifted pleasantly through the open kitchen window.

An enclosed mud room led to a deck in the back, stained year round by tiny plums that fell so furiously in late summer it was impossible to eat them up. Someone had put an ancient claw foot bathtub off the deck in the middle of a tangle of ground cover. In the summer, I plugged the drain and filled it with water from the hose. "Our own swimming pool!" David laughed, jumping in with his trunks on.

Cedar finally had a space of her own, dinky and incongruously attached to the kitchen. "I love my room, Mommy!" She decorated it in a whirlwind of crayoned pictures and stuffed animals propped up on her bookcase and dresser.

Our tiny bedroom was in the front of the house with the head of the bed right against a window that began leaking in the rainy season. "How is that even possible?" I asked Ed. "The entire window is under the front porch." When complaints to the landlord were ignored, we found our own remedies; duct tape and towels.

David's room was a loft, nearly as big as the whole downstairs with a row of windows along one side where he kept a small plastic aquarium with a live clawed frog that never left the water. The shelves underneath were covered with all kinds of keepsakes and ten-year-old boy mulch— comic books, baseballs and star wars collectibles.

Molly loved David's room; she sped up the stairs to the warmth in the winter, and sometimes plopped down on the sliding plexiglass panel that worked like a door between the upstairs and the living room. We had a spectacular view of a smooshed cat tummy from underneath, one that most people never get to see.

Shortly after we moved in, Molly got sick. She stopped eating and became weak so fast we rushed her to the vet in a panic. "She's a fat little cat," Dr. Brown picked her up and bounced her limp form gently up and down above the counter in the waiting room, weighing her in his arms.

Cedar brought her old green baby blanket with the appliquéd turtle to leave with Molly at the hospital. She still slept with it, so this was a sacrifice. "I want Molly to smell me so she won't be scared."

Dr. Brown kept her for the day to run tests and called me that evening. "Mrs. Rosenfield, Molly has a serious liver condition. I'm afraid at this point it will take surgery to save her life."

"Oh no." I asked the looming question. "What would that cost?'

"I'm sorry but it's a rather expensive procedure, close to a thousand dollars. Think it over and let me know your decision," he said kindly, euthanasia gently implied.

"Let's go sit on the front porch steps," I said to the kids. We settled on the top two, listening to the crickets hiding in our little anise field. "The vet just called and told me Molly is pretty sick." I paused, afraid of where the catch in my voice would lead.

"Oh Mommy, what'll happen to her?" Cedar said.

"Well, he told me she needs an operation, but it costs a lot of money. I'm not sure we can afford it." I pulled out a Kleenex and blew my nose.

"We *have* to Mom," David looked at me disbelieving.

"We can't just let her die," Cedar was crying now.

"We won't," I said with more certainty than I felt, wondering what I'd tell Ed.

He understood, of course and we paid for it with a credit card. Molly stayed at the hospital for several more days, and when she got home she was thin and weak, with all the fur shaved off her right side. "She has blue skin!" Cedar said, amazed.

I had to force pills down her throat for another week, opening her mouth and stuffing them halfway down her throat. She would have clawed me to death if she'd had the strength. She was eating again, small amounts of soft food all smashed up in the center of a porcelain dish.

Two weeks later Molly had completely recovered. The only sign of her recent ordeal was baby fine fur and faint stripes growing back in perfect alignment, like a carefully tailored suit.

7

THE MAGIC ZOO

I got calls sometimes from the kids during my work days. It amused my co-workers when David rang me up to ask permission to eat a peach, (this happened frequently in the late spring) or Cedar grabbed the phone away to complain, her little girl voice piping through the receiver, "Mommy, David's teasing me again."

That's why I was unprepared when David, near tears, called to say, "I don't know where Cedar is."

They'd been together at a toy store a block from home when Cedar got mad at David for some reason and walked out. She was seven years old.

"Mom?" David wondered if I were still there. I was, *physically*, but my words were lost, like blind fish swimming circles in a well. "I'm coming home," I finally managed.

"Merry, what's wrong?" my boss, Chris, had excellent radar. I bawled out the story in her office with the door wide open. I didn't care. All she said was "I'm driving you home." We were throwing on coats and grabbing purses when David called back to tell me Cedar had just walked in the door. In an instant, the phrase "flooded with relief" had Technicolor meaning. I collapsed into a chair and said, "Let me talk to her."

"I was mad at David," she told me simply. She had been pouting after her escape and took the long way home, detouring through downtown Mill Valley then back up the hill to our house.

When I got home that night, I lectured them. "You kids know you're supposed to come straight home from school."

"I'm sorry Mom," David apologized, but Cedar was still huffy.

"Cedar, never do anything like that again. I was terrified something had happened to you."

"Mom, I was just walking. I didn't talk to anyone." I pictured her storming past the shops and do-nothing twenty somethings who hung out in the cobble-stoned village square juggling round cloth balls and flirting with each other.

"I don't care. When I'm at work, you stay with your brother."

There were no further incidents, and when I finished my two and a half year contract at the mission, I got a job in a stationary shop in Mill Valley, two blocks from our house. It was in the spring of 1989.

The person who owned the shop was a tall and angular man with a perpetual frown. "Yes, we can use some restocking help. Be on time, nine o'clock tomorrow morning." He glared at me.

But his sourpuss stodginess was undermined by gigantic playboy centerfolds assaulting anyone who ventured into the stockroom downstairs. "Could *he* have put them up?" I wondered. It was unsettling.

I quit after an uncomfortable month, laboring under those posters and his lurking shadow. "It isn't working out for me," I told him, but his expression was unchanged. "Your last check will be ready in a week."

What to do now? I thought about the moonlighting jobs I'd held over the past couple years. While I was still working at the mission, I'd continued with Karen as a long distance jewelry designer. I sent my completed work back to Florida every week and gratefully received payment, which I used for the kids' private school.

During that first year in California I spent the evenings listening to classical music and making jewelry. It was pleasant enough, But Karen decided she wanted all her artists under one roof in Florida.

That's when I went to work for Annie, the mask maker. She was a fortyish bohemian artist with shoulder length blond hair working out of a mobile studio in an impromptu industrial park in Sausalito. I went there once a week to pick up my work before heading to my full-time job in the city. "Hi, Merry, there's no rush on these." She handed me a stack of plaster animal masks and her model to work from. Annie was happy with my work and let me keep any rejects. My five nieces and nephews got them for Christmas that year; child-sized tiger, panther and wolf heads, hand painted and tied in the back with thin, black ribbons.

I liked Annie, the work was fairly creative and she paid well. Now, at age fifty-nine, the thought of two jobs working for other people exhausts me, but I was young then and determined to give our children a good education. Still, I wondered about the neighborhood school just three blocks away. And I thought wistfully of an extra eight hundred dollars in our pockets every month.

"Ed, what do you think about checking out the local elementary school? It seems like it ought to be pretty good in this town." After all, this was affluent, artistic Mill Valley.

"Sure, why not visit it and see?"

The principal was a thin man in a brown tweed suit, with hair receding to a ring that stretched from ear to ear. His face was mild and kind. "So tell me about your children," he smiled at us as if accepting two more children to his school would be his greatest pleasure.

Our children started school there in early spring. They made friends quickly, jumping a hurdle I hadn't realized I'd been worried about. When Cedar learned to read a month later I was sure we had done the right thing.

By the time I had quit my stationary store job they had been in public school for over a year. "If I go back to selling, I've got to be home by three every day," I told Ed that evening.

Some ideas I had been toying with coalesced that night while I slept. The next morning, I picked up a blob of black clay and made a cat with his tail straight in the air, hunched and ready to pounce. I tipped his tail with white and gave him a matching muzzle below two black and copper eyes. Not bad. This one was large, brooch sized. I made a pair of matching earrings, two sitting cats with their tails curled coyly in an impossible but whimsical position.

"That's so cute, Mom!" Cedar had just gotten home from school. "What's it for?"

"I'm going to sell them."

I made frogs, cats, Siamese fighting fish, ladybugs, dogs—even some abstract designs, anything I thought people might buy. Farm animals were popular in the 1980s, so I created a black and white cow head with a pink tongue and a fat round pig with a corkscrew tail. I baked them in our oven and fastened on ear wires and pin backs at the kitchen table.

When I thought I'd made enough, I put them each in a little gold box with the lid on the bottom so you could see the jewelry right away. Those boxes sat in a shallow black cardboard box of which I had three, stacked and held in my arms like school books.

I drove to San Rafael that Friday, parked on the street and walked into the first business, a real estate office. The receptionist looked up at me, smiling automatically. "May I help you?"

"Well, I'm a local artist and I've brought some of my jewelry designs to show you."

It worked! She called the realtors in the back to come up front and they buzzed around my boxes while I slid to the side. My work seemed transformed, magically alluring under five pairs of admiring eyes.

A tall blond woman in a light blue pantsuit held up a pair of cow earrings. "These are adorable! I'll take these and this Siamese cat pin" She paid me thirty-three dollars.

Buoyed, I walked down the street in and out of beauty salons, pet stores, dentists' offices and vet clinics. I didn't skip any door because I didn't know who would buy. I worked about four hours and counted the money. One hundred fifty dollars, as much as I'd made in a week at the stationary store.

My new line of work needed official recognition, as well as a name.

This I made up while I was on my way, (two blocks to go) to fill out forms at the Court House in San Francisco the next day. Before posting a "Doing Business As" announcement in the local paper, I had to be legal.

Magic Circus? Kaleidoscope of Animals? Magic Zoo? Magic Zoo had a certain rhythm. I said it out loud a few times, trying it out on my tongue. I wasn't convinced but thought *I can always change it later* which of course I never did.

8

HIKING

Every weekend we packed the kids into the old brown Toyota station wagon and drove some place where we could walk under trees and over dirt trails. Marin County was full of possibilities.

We hiked on Mt. Tam one Sunday in May. From our parking place in the lot the hills appeared to roll gently, but this was an illusion. After twenty minutes the trail gathered vertical momentum and I was leaning heavily on the front of each thigh with open palms, encouraging my legs to pump their way to the summit. I heard Ed's voice just above me. "Wait till you see this view!"

David and Cedar passed me laughing. "C'mon, Mom!" But I enjoyed my slow climb.

"You miss all the bugs and interesting rocks when you go so fast," I panted when I finally caught up. Ed laughed. I looked out over a reach of grassy swells, pockets of live oak trees nestled in places where the water drained in the rainy season. *Did people see the same thing in this spot a thousand years ago?* I imagined them looking over these same hills, dark intelligent eyes watching for mule deer and rabbit.

We walked down the other side, into the woods. "Look Mom, a sleeping owl" David stage-whispered. The little bird perched directly over the trail, on a limb that reached from one side to the other. "C'mon Cedar, let's see if we can fool him!" They took turns walking under him and squeaking, pretending to be mice.

I turned to Ed, "Look!" but he'd already seen the golden eyes shoot open and focus on our large child prey in one sharp, evaluating head jerk. The next instant his eyes were shut again.

"Squeak, Squeak!" They ran under him, hands held bent and close to their chests, mincing little steps like cartoon mice. The owl didn't learn. Like a windup toy he did the same thing every time; big searching yellow eyes, "Oh, they're too big to eat," and then back to sleep.

Finally I said, "Let's go, kids." I thought the poor bird deserved some pity.

David and Cedar ran ahead looking for the slatted bridge across the creek where they could be trolls to our

Billy goats. They disappeared down the trail and quietly got into position.

I timidly approached the bridge. "Who's that tramping over my bridge?" in unison from the opposite side, a slight alteration of the original tale, where the troll waits under the bridge.

"It's just me, the little Billy Goat Gruff," I said in a tiny voice.

"Then we're coming to EAT you!" they shouted.

"But wait, there's a much bigger Billy goat coming after me!" I scampered safely to the other side.

Ed tramped slowly across the bridge, each footfall as slow and loud as he could make it. He glared maliciously at the trolls. "No!" Cedar shouted and hid behind her brother.

But David was intrepid. "You have to pay us to cross this bridge!" he demanded bravely.

"Oh, all right," said the second Billy Goat Gruff, reaching in his pocket for pennies.

Later that afternoon David spotted a snake on top of a hill, a small constrictor with his body wrapped around a brown mouse twisting to position himself for the swallow. Could he really open his mouth that wide? It seemed impossible but we watched for a long time and sure enough his dislodged jaw got around that rodent, skinny body stretched impossibly for the swallow.

This upset Cedar. "The poor mouse! How can you watch?" she wept.

"If the snake doesn't catch mice to eat he'll starve. And usually they catch the ones that are too sick or old to get away so it helps the mouse family grow stronger." There was a pause while she digested this.

"Are you sure?" she was listening, wanting to believe me.

"Definitely. It's all figured out so everybody in nature has a way to survive. Besides, that mouse may already have a new baby body."

She wiped her tears on her sleeve and I gave her a hug. "Okay, Mommy. If you really think he'll be all right."

"I'm sure of it."

She searched for rocks along the trail, a quiet diversion after the tragedy. Cedar collected them on all our hikes. She'd pick them up along the way, examining them from several angles. They weren't necessarily pretty rocks in the usual sense, but all of them had interesting shapes or colors. "Mom, can you carry this rock?" she would ask because she wore those pocketless stretch pants that all seven-year-old girls loved in the late 1980s.

Her most spectacular rock find occurred that day, on the way back to the car. It was a heavy bluish-green stone that we later discovered had magnetic powers. "Cedar, you have to carry it part of the way yourself," I told her. It was an

exciting find and she didn't complain as she clutched it to
her childish bosom and staggered a few yards down the trail.

"Okay, Sweetie, I'll take it now," Ed told her, smiling.

It was dusk and our car sat alone in the parking lot.
The kids flopped into the back seat exhausted, smelling of
fresh air and dirt.

9

TERRY AND PETER

Ed's ex-wife Terry had lived in San Francisco since 1970, where she raised their son Peter by herself. For many years, she and I had a bare acquaintanceship.

In 1967, Ed and Terry had met while flying back to college after summer break. By accident they were seated next to each other where Ed could admire close up Terry's fresh-faced beauty and good legs. Terry looked right into Ed's dark brown eyes and dreamed about an affair with this good-looking stranger. She told me later he reminded her of Omar Sharif.

When the plane landed, they spent the remainder of that sexually charged day together and one romantic night during which they conceived a child.

Six weeks later Terry arrived on Ed's campus from hers to announce the result of their passionate but unprotected night. Despite intense parental chagrin on both sides and the difficulties of remaining in architecture school under vastly altered circumstances, Ed made Terry his bride. Ed was twenty-two years old and Terry only nineteen when Peter was born, in March of 1968, a curly-headed blond cherub. I know the baby Peter from faded photos of him being held by Ed's aging parents and one of pretty young Terry smiling faintly, holding little Peter in her lap with Ed sitting next to them looking as if he were already on his way someplace else.

Ed dropped out of architecture school and the little family traveled to San Francisco in a VW bus, joining the ranks of westward bound young people leaving behind their middle class upbringing for something they predicted would be much bigger and more important.

By the time Peter was a toddler, Ed had begun experimenting with Eastern spirituality and psychedelic drugs. This strained their already tenuous marriage and in 1971, they divorced. Ed left San Francisco, but Terry made it her permanent home.

I met Peter the same night I met Ed, at a party in Kansas City in the spring of 1974. My singing partner Andy and I had just performed at a folk club called, *The Fool Killer*. Andy was a self-proclaimed tall skinny kid with glasses, a close friend from high school. Back in those early days, he was the only person I knew who smoked pot and observed the world in such a delightfully skewed way.

Andy had a beautiful baritone voice more suited to Broadway musicals than the traditional Appalachian and British Isles folk music we sang in tender harmonies. But he had moved to Wichita, Kansas from Ohio on a whim and within two weeks we were performing together locally.

The post-concert party was in full swing—musicians and folk music fans gathered in groups throughout the two-story Victorian near the club. But I was sipping a glass of red wine, sitting alone on an itchy wool couch, new in 1930. An olive-skinned man with long black hair that hung in ringlets around his face watched me silently from across the room. He was dressed in a pair of denim coveralls, shirtless underneath.

He has good biceps. My boozy mind was wandering. *I wonder if he's attracted to me?* At this party, like every other social gathering I attended in my early twenties, I had high hopes of finding my true love.

The handsome stranger walked across the room, sat down next to me and asked a question, quietly, and right in my ear.

"I'm sorry. I couldn't hear what you said." Three musicians were singing a loud, lusty ballad ten feet away in the adjoining room, completely drowning out his words.

"Do you want to come home with me?" He spoke up this time.

I blushed unexpectedly but answered, "Okay." *Maybe he's the one I've been searching for.*

Besides the overalls, Ed wore John Lennon glasses and earth shoes, popular in those days of unfashionable fashion. It was an overall look I approved of. We were gathering our things, getting ready to leave when he detoured to the kitchen.

"This is my son, Peter," he introduced me to the six-year-old playing with a pair of kittens under the table.

A son? I was momentarily anguished. A boyfriend with a child did not fit into my romanticized future. I smiled anyway. "Hello, Peter."

"Hi." He looked disappointed too.

As we climbed into Ed's 1957 Pontiac, Peter turned to his dad and asked, "Why is *she* coming home with us?"

Ed put Peter to bed in the room next to us, and we enjoyed a passionate, if reckless night of romance.

The next morning Peter jumped on the bed before we had risen. Ed sprung up, swung Peter around the room and sang *Too Much Monkey Business,* a Chuck Berry song.

Ed would be my second real boyfriend. I'd had only a few former affairs, and most of those hardly qualified— men who had watched me perform at a club, or fellow musicians. I believed that sleeping with admiring strangers would lead me to my soul mate. This, contrary to all common sense, is exactly what happened.

Ed no longer took drugs. He was involved in a spiritual philosophy I had never heard of called Scientology. This added to his mystique.

In Wichita I lived in a communal house with Andy and three other young people. Since our first night together I had gone back to Kansas City on the Greyhound to visit once and Ed had come to see me one Friday night a month later, carrying the sleeping Peter in his arms. By now I had gotten used to the idea of dating a father. And I had discovered that Peter was a sweet kid, smart and funny.

"Look at the color in your cheeks!' Andy teased me the morning after one especially rapturous night.

Ed and I were mostly apart, but affectionate letters drifted back and forth. I noted he had signed his last one, "Love." This I opened and read so many times the paper in the fold had gotten soft.

When it was time to drive Peter back to San Francisco a month later, Ed asked me to come with him.

I was afraid he would never return, and was appalled at the self-inflicted drama of having to choose between my life as a budding musician and this new romance. Andy and I had a growing following of fans and since we were performing now on television and radio locally, I thought fame was close to hand.

Was I in love? I ignored the doubt and barely acknowledged the question. Ed was attracted to me, a novel and exciting development. Andy was upset and brusque toward Ed, easing me further away from our duo.

"I don't know what to do!" I wailed. Ed and I sat on the front porch step, his arm around my shoulders. I poured out my grief and worry, but it was Ed's quiet kindness that helped me choose the right direction.

The day before we left I took my savings out of the bank, all six hundred fifty dollars. I'd put it aside from working at my day job in the hospital kitchen, plus tip and gig money squirreled away from playing music. I hugged Andy goodbye, feeling guilty and a little lost. "It'll work out," he said smiling, mentally moving onto bigger things already. Andy recovered quickly and within a year had created an *industrial strength dance band* called The Moderns. They even made an album. "I've made it on to vinyl!" he proudly told me over the phone two years later.

Ed bought an old brown rambler station wagon for fifty dollars to replace the Pontiac, which had perished from an ignition fire two weeks earlier. His ability to pick a good engine in an old beater was new to me, and I stared at it bleakly. "It runs like a dream," he assured me, giving the hood a pat.

By the next day, the dry Colorado wind was blowing our hair into tangled knots. I sat next to Ed with my hand resting on his knee, saying little and worrying quietly. I was sure if he discovered who I *really* was he'd be flooded with second thoughts, such as, *She has such a weird sense of humor—and so brooding. How could I have missed those obvious warning signs?* Now this seems hard to believe, because of all the people in the world Ed has loved me steadfastly these thirty-five years and is the only person I eventually felt safe enough to confide in completely. But youth and uncertainty made me fear this delicate balance of lovemaking and reality would come to an explosive end.

After three days we arrived in California. Terry lived on the top floor of an old house in Oakland with a man named Michael. The front yard had the largest century plant I'd ever seen, blue green daggers reaching almost as high as Terry's windows and a flower stem in the middle as thick as a large man's wrist.

When she opened the door, Peter dashed to her and Terry squatted at his level, squeezing him so tightly I wondered how she had given him up, even for a summer. I felt out of place. "Hello," we shook hands awkwardly, but that was because circumstances made friendship at first sight impossible.

Ed and I drove back to the Midwest, renting an apartment in the Italian section of town in Kansas City. Our landlady, who lived next door, grew plum tomatoes in the back yard and I could smell the slow-cooking sauce from our open bedroom window on cool fall days. Did she know we weren't married? That worried me a little.

Ed drove a truck for a produce company and I got a job waitressing in a diner a few blocks away. I wanted to play music again, but the only other musician I knew in town was a man named Tim who surprised me with a call one afternoon, asking if I wanted to jam. "I want to meet with him and see if we can work out some stuff!" I told Ed, flattered.

"I don't think you should do that." Ed knew him from the coffeehouse and told me, darkly, that he was a known scoundrel. I called him back to cancel, but still pined to perform.

I quit my job, tired of low pay and long hours. During a lull in job hunting, I picked up Ed's copy of *Dianetics the Modern Science of Mental Health* by L. Ron Hubbard. I'm sure I missed more than I absorbed in that first reading, but it still intrigued me.

"Is there someplace in Kansas City I could take a class?" Ed and I were eating dinner—cheese enchiladas, brown rice and pinto beans. We were slim but shared a dozen enchiladas for a meal; seven for Ed and five for me. And topped it off with a root beer float!

"Yes, there's a Scientology mission not too far from here. We could drive down there this weekend if you want to check it out."

"Yes, I'd like that."

My first class was called the Communication Course, consisting of some theory and a series of drills to work on with another student. "This is fun!" I announced to Ed after my first evening. I swallowed any thoughts of being done with study, an idea I'd settled on after dropping out of college four years earlier. This new subject really intrigued me!

There was an open mike at a well-known folk club in one of Kansas City's new hip districts that weekend. "I want to go." I told Ed, who was happy I'd found a reason to perform again.

I wasn't a bit nervous, so when I stepped onstage I knew something had already changed. Back in Wichita I always did our gigs a little tipsy, which I thought calmed me down and made me sound better. But now I was completely sober with absolutely no stage fright. Not only that, but performing felt more like a *conversation* with the audience, instead of an attempt to overwhelm them with my singing voice. "Merry, you were incredible!" Ed, my biggest fan, hugged me afterwards.

"I can't believe how much fun that was!" I said, grinning.

Ed and I lived in Kansas City for another year, but we longed to move somewhere near mountains. When Ed's father passed away later that year, we packed our belongings and headed toward Flagstaff, Arizona. There was a small Scientology center there at the time and we continued our courses under the benign shadow of the San Francisco Peaks.

The following summer, Ed and I kept Peter with us in Flagstaff, where we spent the year before our marriage living in a mobile home with the fragrant, piney National Forest as our backyard. When Terry surprised us with a visit on the back of her boyfriend's motorcycle that July, she put me in my place as a potential stepmother. "Peter's shoes have holes in them and it looks like he never bathes." She was hurt more than critical, and I was humiliated. I hadn't noticed the holes, but bathing was a sore spot between Peter and me.

"I don't want to take a bath. I'm not dirty!" I didn't know how to get around his flat refusal without using force, being years away from perfecting the maternal art of cajoling.

After that summer visit, Terry and I had little contact for the next ten years. But in 1987, when our family moved to Mill Valley, we were just a few miles from the apartment where she and Peter lived in San Francisco. We had talked a few times on the phone over the past year.

After work one day I called her to ask a favor, as good a way as any to break the ice, I thought. "Terry, this is Merry! Can you go shopping with me? I have to buy a semi-formal dress for a party and I have no idea where to find one in this city."

"Sure. I know just the place." She sounded happy to hear from me.

She waited for me after work me in her little Honda Accord. Terry was still a very pretty woman and wore her now strawberry blond hair pulled back in a long French braid. She had wide, cornflower blue eyes. "Do you want to hear some of my boyfriend's music?" she asked, poised with the tape in front of the deck.

"Oh, sure," I said, dreading having to pretend enthusiasm. She clicked it into place and the tape whirred to her boyfriend's voice, which filled the car with big gravely sound, soulful and compelling. "He's incredible!" I shouted, surprised.

"I know," she said.

We listened quietly for fifteen minutes. It wasn't quite blues, but his words, melody and harmonica had that sort of bone-deep humanity and depth. "Terry, this is wonderful stuff. Tell me about this guy."

"His name is Rick Hatfield and we met in Wichita where he lives…"

"Wichita? What a coincidence!" I interrupted.

"Oh yes, that's where you were living when you met Ed. Anyway, we had one date and discovered during the conversation that both of us had taken classes in Scientology in the past, and both of us had separately realized how much we missed it and wanted to get back on a course. Amazing, huh?"

We chattered on the rest of the afternoon, stopping only at the outlet store with the gigantic dressing room full of frantic females trying on and discarding formerly expensive dresses with this one last chance before being carted to thrift stores. I found a beautiful bluish-green and black fitted one with a wide belt, calf length. "It emphasizes your waist," Terry pointed out, eyeing me from all angles. I looked at the price tag. It was originally seventy-five dollars, pretty expensive for 1986. The sale price – fifteen dollars!

"I'll take it."

Terry drove me back to Mill Valley.

"You know, we do have some things in common." She looked at me sideways while driving under the rainbow bridge. "We're both artists."

"Yep, and we both have beautiful sons by the same father." We laughed.

"The main reason I have Peter is because I took one look at Ed and knew he would make a beautiful baby."

"That makes sense to me, especially since you were only nineteen at the time."

When we got to the street below our house, I thanked Terry and we hugged. "Do you and Peter want to come over for Thanksgiving?" I asked.

"Sure, we'd love to!"

That Thanksgiving was our first extended family event and Cedar was curious. "Were you married to my dad before?"

"Yes, a long time ago," Terry laughed.

"So Peter is our brother," David pointed out, but I don't think Cedar believed him. After dinner we sat in the living room, on the floor. Peter played his guitar and I lifted my dulcimer from its wooden case and sang *McPherson's Lament*.

Peter was now eighteen. He'd grown into a slim, good-looking young man with curly blond hair worn a little long. His eyes were brown and kind like his dad's, and his nose long and straight, a curious genetic mixture of Ed and

Terry's. He was a tremendously good guitar player, mostly electric rock, but that day he accompanied me quietly.

A few months later, Terry called me after work, her voice soft, almost a whisper. "I've just found out I have breast cancer."

"Oh Terry."

"Remember when I told you about that lump I'd found? They did a biopsy and the doctor told me I need to have a radical mastectomy. They think the cancer is already in my lymph nodes." She paused, trying not to cry. "I've been so happy and now I wonder if I'll be alive in two weeks." I remembered innocently reassuring her a week earlier, telling her it was probably nothing, but to get the lump checked out anyway. I shook my head, eyes welling and grateful she couldn't see me. Terry was only thirty-nine.

I was at the hospital in San Francisco when she came out of surgery. I walked into the recovery room where she lay on a high bed with rails, looking frail and tired. A gigantic white bandage was where her left breast had been. "It doesn't hurt," was the first thing she said to me, which was the most surprising thing. I held her hand and asked her what she needed. "Just talk to me."

Rick moved to San Francisco while she recuperated. He was a short man, solid, with curly auburn hair and freckled arms. The first thing he said to me made me laugh.

"You are an incredible musician!" I blurted out. He came come back with something that was unprintable, but hysterically funny.

I was happy he was with Terry, who looked noticeably brighter since his arrival.

Peter had a girlfriend now, Kari — a jolly, buxom girl with a faint London accent. She had peaches-and-cream skin and wore her red hair cropped short. She and Peter lived with Terry, but were looking for a place of their own in Marin County.

Terry loved our children and once told me, "I feel like I finally have a daughter." When she was better, she took care of them occasionally, once giving Ed a special birthday gift, a romantic get-a-way with me at a hot spring resort in the Northern California countryside.

When Rick's gigs were at family-friendly places, we brought our kids to hear him play. At a Pizzeria in Sausalito, Terry sat next to our family, close to the stage. I watched her giggle quietly while he teased her gently through one entire song about "chicken legs," a private joke between them.

"He makes me laugh," Terry said.

10

$\int$ ALAMANDER$\int$

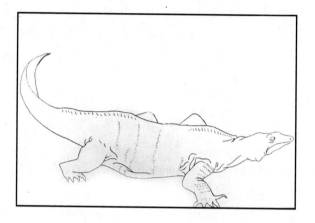

One of our weekend hikes took us down Tennessee Valley Road in Mill Valley, all the way to trail's end at the Pacific. It wasn't a swimming beach, but we loved the drama of slate grey waves foaming and crashing at the very edge of California.

David and Cedar ran ahead of us, hiding behind grass and hills along the wide trail and popping out to surprise us, a game they invented when we lived in Oakland where they used cars and hedges instead. "Run ahead and see if we can find you!" Ed and I encouraged them, allowing us kidless minutes to talk privately.

In the spring I watched for salamanders along the way. "Hey mom, come here! I found one!" The kids helped me out, scouting ahead on the parallel stream. They were reddish, rubbery-looking amphibians that swam away with their limbs held against their sides like tiny sleek alligators.

On the first flat part of the walk families moseyed with strollers and little kids bundled up or in bathing suits depending on the weather. We all nodded to each other, young families trying to wear out their children, retired people holding hands and young lovers walking close, smooching.

Near the end of the walk and before we got to the beach was a marshy area to the right of the trail. Red-winged blackbirds dodged frantically, flashing brilliant crimson under glossy black wing feathers. They called "Ok-a **lee**", a bouncy sound like a musical spring, probably warning their friends about us.

"Did you know you could eat cattail roots?" Ed asked the kids.

"Really? Have you ever eaten one?" David was interested.

"Yes, in New Mexico once." Several years before I met Ed he was a hippie in a small New Mexican town. He went by the name of "Ojito Ed" and had a dapple-grey horse he taught himself to ride. Sometimes he'd walk for hours to see his closest neighbors, a woman named Mary, her two lovers and their three offspring.

"What do cattails taste like?" David asked. Cedar had lost interest and was wandering down to the edge of the pond, perhaps searching for more salamanders.

"They're kind of bland, not too bad. Pretty good if you're starving, though."

"Can we pick one?"

"I don't think we're supposed to pull up plants here, we'd better not."

"Okay. Can we go to the beach now?" David was an easygoing kid.

The last third of the walk was the steep part; brick red trails with low-lying vegetation off to the right. "Slow down you guys, and pay attention!" Kicked stones tumbled to the left, falling hollowly down the side.

We smelled the water before we saw it. There were craggy rocks at the back perimeter and the sand was coarse, studded with driftwood and people. I was shivering, fooled again by the micro-climatic change from our yard to the beach. "I'm freezing," I complained.

Ed shook his head in mock disgust. "I can't believe you forgot your sweater again." But he gave me his jacket anyway.

We plopped on dry sand, squinting toward our children who were off to explore whatever washed up that day. The Pacific was too cold for a dip without a wet suit, but was perfect for walking in the dark sand right by the waves.

Cedar squealed when she got too close, bare feet caught unaware by reaching fingers of foam.

"Cedar, let's build a sand castle!" David waved something in the air toward his sister, a big stick for a digging tool. We could still hear the rhythm and tone of their voices but their words were drowned by sea noise.

"This is so nice," I looked toward the horizon and dug an indentation in the sand with a ridged shell the size of my thumbnail. Ed's eyes were shut under his straw fedora and I reached for his hand.

11

THE EARTHQUAKE

I was at home by myself when the house started to shake on that October day in 1989. There was nowhere to go. It wasn't like being caught in a thunderstorm where you can run under something or even a hurricane when a closet stuffed with mattresses might keep you safe.

There was a rumbling roar from somewhere far beneath where I stood. In those seconds of terror I pictured behemoth rocks deep in the earth trying impossibly to squeeze past each other. My reaction was immediate; I ran outside in time to see Molly still in her "meatloaf" position on the railing of the porch looking wild-eyed while the railing pitched crazily under her belly.

I must have looked funny, taking a few steps toward the stairs that separated houses on our hill, glancing back towards Molly still trembling on the railing, looking up wistfully because of this urge to go *up*, off the planet. An airplane was flying to San Francisco or just passing over it. Passengers, faraway pin-points of awareness, enjoyed their coffee or dreamt about their destinations. All these thoughts happened within seconds, when my own survival seemed most at risk.

The earth became placid after fifteen or so seconds *was that all?* and I thought about where my family was.

Ed and David were both in San Francisco, and since the earthquake had happened in Mill Valley (I assumed) I wasn't worried about them.

But Cedar! Cedar was at a friend's house where she'd gone after school, an apartment a few blocks away. I ran there, cursing my mental and physical slowness. I couldn't see any damage along the way, but I watched buildings and electrical wires warily.

The girls answered the door flushed and excited. "Mommy, there was an *earthquake*!" Cedar said happily. Tara's mother wasn't home, I realized, annoyed.

I waited with the girls till she returned and took everyone back to our house, walking slowly this time. "Where's your husband?" I asked Rashida.

"He's traveling now, for business. When I spoke with him last night he had just arrived in New York. He'll be so worried." Cedar and Tara danced ahead of us, chattering excitedly.

"I'm glad we were inside, but the telephone poles looked so funny when they leaned over!" The girls giggled.

As soon as we stepped in the door I tried to call Ed at work and got a recording that the lines were tied up, with only emergency calls getting through. I turned on the radio in the kitchen and listened, horrified, to descriptions of buildings in San Francisco caving in and the collapse of the Bay Bridge.

This is what Cedar wrote in her diary that night:

"Today we had an earthquake! The Bay Bridge fell down! I was home alone playing dress up with Tara and then our moms came in the house and saved us, or that is what they think. Then we all went to my house and ate Chinese food but I had to do my homework."

My thoughts were elsewhere, not on entertaining my guests nor on making sure Cedar did her homework. *Where were David and Ed?*

With only the alarming radio news as a gauge, my images were of Ed and David calling feebly for help under piles of rubble, injured, maybe near death. It sounded like half of San Francisco was in ruins.

But they were only trying to drive home, through traffic snarled all the way from San Francisco to way past

Novato. Hours later they arrived to grateful hugs and the Chinese carry-out that Cedar mentioned.

When I talked to Terry the following day she told me about her harrowing escape down seventeen floors on a wobbly fire escape in downtown San Francisco. She was working in one of the largest towers when it began to sway, pens and telephone sliding from her desk and women screaming in the office next door. The lights went off and the only way to get out of there safely was down the side like cat woman.

No one we knew personally had been injured, but one of Cedar's classmates lost a father in the bridge collapse.

12

RADIO SHOWS

Someone back in California did a wonderful thing and put old radio shows on one of the local stations in the evenings. We discovered them by accident on a drive back with the kids from Pt. Reyes one Saturday night.

David and Cedar became instant Jack Benny fans. They were fascinated by Rochester's gravelly voice and Jack Benny's exasperation. The kids laughed so hard they would have missed the next line, but those old Vaudeville comics knew how to leave time for that.

There were other great shows. *George Burns and Gracie Allen, Charley McCarthy, Lights Out.* That was a scary one, perfect for the dark car ride home.

They didn't edit out the commercials, which made that forty year time gap more real, because the humor in the shows wasn't at all dated. I'm pretty sure cigarette commercials were already off the air in the late 1980s, so *Lucky Strike Means Fine Tobacco* (LSMFT) seemed quaint, from an era when every glamorous star smoked.

We listened to them every weekend and the old radio shows became part of what our kids grew up on.

13

THE DEBUT

In second grade, Cedar began to develop her writing skills, creating scary stories and mysteries.

My favorite one is *The Case of the Crowing Bird*, a work of fiction told in the first person. *"I heard a bird singing in the tree that seemed to be trying to tell me something and in the middle of the night I heard it again! But this time it sounded more dangerous, like it belonged to a witch or something. I looked it up in a bird book, but it was not in there so I looked in another book it said a new type of bird was coming to town. In the day it sounds kind of weird and in the night it sounds wicked and like it belongs to a witch and in the night it is very, very dangerous. But it can not harm you unless you look at it more than a minute."*

We seldom went to movies (never scary movies) and of course had no TV for this kind of inspiration.

She also wrote poetry:

The Moon

Big, Round

Moving, Waxing, Waning

The Moon is high

Space

She was given an assignment to describe herself and this is what she wrote:

Me

Inside of me there are rivers and green grass, and flowers and rocks and trees.

There are people there are houses and a road and leaves.

One of her mystery stories from that time is about a little girl named Marianne whom nobody liked.

"She made friends with a girl named Merry," wrote Cedar. *"But one day she had a fight with Merry and this is what happened:*

'Merry' said Marianne 'Do you like cats?'

'No!' said Merry. 'I do' said Marianne.

'Then I hate you!' said Merry.

And from that day Marianne was never heard of again."

Her early stories had to be read carefully because rivers were *"revers"* and houses were *"howses"*. Her teacher was exciting; a young woman with short red hair who understood the tenderness of eight-year-old artists and didn't blunt their creativity with endless spelling and grammar corrections. She had each child keep a journal of their thoughts, written to her on a weekly basis. She answered each entry respectfully, as if she were communicating to a peer. I thought she was perfect for Cedar, but trouble with spelling dogged Cedar thereafter. Looking back I think it was a small price to pay.

Hanging in my studio now is a watercolor painting Cedar did this same year. It lay folded in my closet for over thirteen years, but *Someday*, I thought, *I will frame this.*

The background is midnight blue. A perfectly circular sun, black rays circling it like too many fat spiders' legs, shines in the upper right corner. It's poised over a scene of multi-hued buildings, fences and cars. Three white clouds outlined in black float across the top, high above the buildings in a barely descending row. Cedar handed it to me in our kitchen after school one day. "Mommy, this is for you." She had a serious face. This was a gift crafted carefully over days of art class.

"Oh Cedar, it's *beautiful*," I said honestly.

For the grade school "Spring Fling" that May, Cedar's second-grade class performed an excerpt from *Alice in Wonderland*. Cedar was cast in the role of The Mad Hatter.

In the third row back, Ed and I perched tensely on two metal folding chairs. Both our kids would be on stage that night. Twelve-year-old David was the narrator and he stood on the right side of the stage, just outside the red velvet curtains. When he spoke, his voice was clear and strong, completely absent of the preadolescent octave slides that had been dogging him for a month. "He doesn't look a bit nervous," I whispered to Ed.

The place was packed with parents and older siblings and it was starting to get hot. When the curtains closed and opened again on a tea party scene, all the actors were in place except for Cedar. There was a commotion, off to the right where steps led from the audience floor to the stage. There she was! I realized with startled disappointment, that Cedar was refusing to go on. And she was crying. What could have gone wrong? Being the Mad Hatter was all Cedar had talked about for the past two weeks. I made my way over to the side of the audience where she was now marching down the aisle towards the back and scooped her up in my arms. When I asked her what happened she shook her head and said "Nothing," in a shaking voice, tears streaming down her face. I didn't notice how the children on stage improvised with the main character absent.

It was an unexplained and mysterious blip at the dawn of her performance career.

14

CHANGE

I was incredulous. "Los Angeles?" Ed hinted at another change while dressing for work that morning, but this was the first time we'd been able to talk about it privately, with the kids tucked in bed.

"I'm afraid it's either there or back to Florida." In two months his contract with the mission in San Francisco would be up, and our main purpose in living here would slip away. Ed was an excellent counselor; he had saved marriages, gotten teenagers back on track and helped people deal with tragedies that had swallowed their lives. I knew he deserved this opportunity to hone his skills but I loved our tucked away life and wasn't feeling reasonable.

We were sitting on the bed with the door shut. I kicked off my shoes and lay down, pressing the heel of my palms over my eyes. "I really hate L.A. How am I going to make money there? It's painful enough selling door to door in Marin County. What about the kids? They have friends and a school they love."

"I suppose I could go by myself..." Ed was sympathetic.

"That's a terrible idea!"

"Merry, you can study there too, you know. It's been a while since you've taken a Scientology class."

He was right. It *was* my spiritual journey, too. "Yes, but it's so hard to think of leaving." Images of Terry, Mt. Tam, trips to Pt. Reyes sharpened and blurred.

"Come here." Ed hugged me. "It'll be fine. Afterwards, we'll move back north."

"It always works out," he finished.

Two months later I wrote this in my journal, right before we left:

"Boxes filled with years of accumulations are appearing here and there in our little house. I have tightness in my chest that threatens to become full blown grief. Terry has grown into one of those few and very special people that are always friends..."

Cedar's diary was more pragmatic:

"I will be moving to L.A. because my parents have to do work there. It will be fun but I don't know what Molly my cat will think of it."

We towed our Toyota behind the U-Haul, full of plants, suitcases and the cat.

We had planned to travel with Molly riding on our laps in the cab, but she would have none of it. "Ouch!" She scratched David in her desperate leap toward the side window and freedom just before we pulled into traffic.

"Kids, we'll have to tow her in the car behind us."

"But Mommy, she'll be so scared!" Cedar's eyes were pleading.

"She'll do fine, probably settle down on the seat and fall asleep." We put a litter box, dry food and a bowl of water on the floor of the car, and checked on her at every rest stop we made along the way.

When we filled up the gas tank David watched her through the car window. "She's panting!"

"We'll roll the window down another inch so she has more air."

At one rest area we took her out on a leash so she could explore her surroundings. She hunched her shoulders, lowered her head and slipped backwards from her collar, disappearing into the brush on the hillside. "Molly!" Cedar screamed. I lunged for her, grabbing her before she could shoot across the parking lot.

"Silly cat, where were you going?" We were only a couple hours from L.A. and the house Ed had rented in La Crescenta a week earlier. "Pretty soon you can check out your new pad, but for now…" I opened the door to the Toyota and she leapt huffily onto the back seat.

We pulled into the driveway of our freshly painted generically suburban home. It was late afternoon so we unloaded all our furniture and boxes while five silent children stared at us from across the street. That night Cedar sobbed for hours with her door shut. "I miss Mill Valley!" I was heartbroken for her.

She went through a succession of three schools before we found one where she was happy, and that was a private school that we could hardly afford but it did have dance and art programs.

David settled into the local public Junior High and as usual was agreeable and uncomplaining; although later he told me there was a girl in his science class that spit on him every day. He seldom studied but continued getting As.

On our day off we took trips to the dry mountains that ringed our desert bowl. We hiked on trails of brittle grass, under pine trees yellowing from the smog that settled up that high. "Look, a flowering yucca!" I pointed out to the kids, ignoring a discarded Pamper blown onto its base.

After we had been back in L.A. for a few months, Terry and Peter came to visit us in the middle of the week. They were on their way to Mexico where Terry was receiving alternative cancer treatment, supposedly complementing the chemo her oncologist in San Francisco was giving her. She said "My doctor hasn't even mentioned the IV marks on my forearm. Maybe he assumes I'm a heroin addict."

Terry and I were working on a long distance project. She was creating T-shirts to go with my jewelry, hand blocked in rich colors and her own creative versions of my designs. Some of her shirts had humorous cartoons that she and Rick had come up with together and had nothing to do with my jewelry. Like this one, for example: A gentleman in a business suit stepping out the front door with his hand held out as if to catch something. He turns to his wife and says *"It looks like rain, Dear"* while six reindeer tumble from the sky behind them.

The two exhibitions we did that Saturday and Sunday were sad affairs - a cat show and a women's club luncheon. I think we made two hundred fifty dollars between us. I have photographs we took of our booth, a table top display with giant cut-out people wearing Terry's shirts, a Magic Zoo beaded necklace slung around its neck and the matching earrings dangling from holes in the cardboard ears.

But while the first show was still a pleasant hopeful on the next day's horizon, we took Terry and Peter to the Gene Autry Western Heritage Museum. We were given little round green and white buttons of a cowboy on a bucking bronco to wear as souvenirs. The museum was perfect for Terry, who loved western art and culture.

Terry and I were happy during the mostly uninterrupted exhibit show hours. We gossiped about our families and futures. "Pete and Kari moved to Marin County," she told me, looking relieved. The city apartment had been crowded with all four of them sardined in. "Rick is playing at Fisherman's Wharf everyday and he's starting to get some good paying gigs too."

"Cool. Sounds like everything is going in the right direction. We'll be moving to Los Gatos when Ed finishes up. He joined staff at the mission there so we'll be fairly close. Not so close as Mill Valley, but a pretty short drive from San Francisco."

On Monday we hugged and waved goodbye as Terry and Peter piled in her Toyota truck with a homemade lunch to see them to Mexico. "We'll be back north before you know it!" I shouted as they drove off, blowing kisses.

15

MARY MARTIN

One Christmas my sister sent a video of the Peter Pan TV special starring Mary Martin, as a gift for David and Cedar. It was a piece of *our* childhood, and I had no idea the effect it would have on one of my own children.

Cedar brought it with her whenever we visited Terry and Rick, to watch on their VCR. She wrote this in her diary:

"I love dance—that's what I will be when I grow up and I will be Peter Pan. I want to fly so much! And I know every song in Peter Pan and I never want to grow up! The only thing I'm looking forward to is driving, and being Peter Pan in the play."

Cedar and I went to see Cathy Rigby in that role when she performed at the Pantages Theatre on Hollywood Boulevard. in 1990. The first glimpse of Peter entering through the Darling's nursery window, the tiny pinpoints of light against the black void and the glorious music that ushered her graceful flight made my eyes fill with tears.

Cedar enjoyed it, but I think to her no one could play that part as well as Mary Martin. She became a Mary Martin fanatic and had tapes of all the musicals she performed in, plus an old deco recording of her singing songs from the 1930s. This was before the Internet, and now when I Google *Mary Martin* I find so many more things Cedar would have loved.

Later that year, I was filling my back seat with groceries when I heard someone mention on the radio that Mary Martin had died. It had happened a month earlier, but we weren't newspaper readers. *Oh no,* I thought, dreading telling Cedar.

"I'm home, Sweetie," I called upstairs after I'd put away the groceries.

"Did you bring me something good?"

"How about a ripe banana?" I teased.

"How about a brownie?" she asked hopefully.

"No, but we can make some zucchini bread tonight after dinner."

She smiled at me. "OK Mommy." Then, "Is there something wrong?" She had a sensitive antenna. I don't think I'd even frowned.

"Let's go sit in the living room."

We settled on the overstuffed grey couch as Molly jumped into her lap. "What is it?" She was a little annoyed, her way of cushioning bad news.

"As I was leaving the grocery store I had the radio on the news. I learned that Mary Martin died in November."

"Oh no, Mommy, how can that be?" She started crying and was petting Molly rhythmically for comfort.

"She'd been ill for a while and her body finally gave out. I'm so sorry." I hugged her.

She wiped her eyes on her sleeves. "I think I'll go to my room." She spent the next hour listening to her tape of *Annie Get Your Gun* from 1957, a recording she had recently bought with her allowance.

Not long afterwards we found a paperback copy of Mary's autobiography in a thrift store. It was dog-eared and autographed in Martin's fast and sloppy scroll, the result of some weary book signing years earlier. It had traveled from *Betty* to Cedar, who now carried it tenderly home to read.

I haven't heard "South Pacific" in years, but since both Cedar and I learned all the words to all the songs, even the ones Mary Martin didn't sing, I can still hum them without hesitation. Cedar, in her exuberantly pitch-challenged alto sang them with such gusto and volume that staying on key myself took intense focus.

It stumped me that the ability to sing on key eluded this talented child. When Cedar was fourteen, I worked with her to learn a song, note by note, for an audition. She fretted over it for weeks, working to memorize every note as if it were a line in a play. When her audition slot arrived, I sat in the dark theatre silently mouthing each word in perfect pitch, willing her to make it through without sharps or flats. She did pretty well considering the pressure involved singing in front of evaluating strangers.

"You did great!" I hugged her afterwards.

She said "Did I stay on key?"

Either my praise was too much or the response was a millisecond too long. Without a word from me, she sulked, slumping in the car seat on the way home.

I was miserable, feeling like a failure myself. I had no idea how to teach someone to sing. It was too easy for me, like walking.

In desperation I started my pep talk. "Look, you did a great job. Your energy on stage was fantastic. So what if a note slipped a little here or there? It makes no difference. Besides, even professional singers mess up once in a while."

"Yeah?" she was listening.

"Yeah" I said with confidence and that was the end of it. Besides, she did get a part in the play she was trying out for. It even involved singing, as part of a group. She did this by mouthing the words silently and no one, not even the director, ever knew.

16

BACK NORTH

Ed and I were almost done with our classes. We had been in L.A. close to a year this time and the prospect of returning north loomed happily. I had already started putting things in boxes.

On my fortieth birthday that November, the nine year old Cedar said "I'm going to buy your dinner." It is a touching memory. Her expression was serious as she carefully counted out her allowance money to treat me. I started to protest then knew there was no way I could deny her this.

We ate at a Japanese restaurant I was fond of, where kimonoed waitresses brought David and Cedar little origami paper animals while the food was being prepared.

My sushi was delivered on a beautifully lacquered bowl that looked like a boat. I mixed soy sauce and wasabi in perfect ratio, hot enough for a quick burst of sinus pain. I breathed in quickly, eyes watering. "Add some more soy sauce," Ed advised. Ed and I had the same meal, besides the sushi a steaming bowl of miso soup and a tiny white dish of sesame scented seaweed. David and Cedar dug into plates of teriyaki chicken and piled white rice, a rare switch from the nutty brown version I always cooked at home.

The following month, Christmas day afternoon, we hastily took down our tree and loaded the moving van. Most years my Christmas memories are of happy kids and toasting waffles, but what I remember from that year was looking for someplace to eat a holiday dinner during our exodus from L.A. The only restaurant open was a Jack-in-the-Box and we ate there hurriedly, huddled at a plastic table. The restaurant was full of sullen teenagers in hooded sweatshirts and glum, overweight families eating in silence.

Ed had a job waiting for him in Los Gatos at the Scientology Mission near downtown. We stayed with friends while we looked for a place to live, and three days later we rented a two story townhouse built in the 1970s. It had modern touches like tall slanted ceilings that ate up your heat in the winter, and a tiny back yard separating you from your neighbors with a low picket fence.

We threw unpacked possessions inside on New Year's Eve day, then drove to Larkspur in Marin County for a holiday dinner at Pete and Kari's place. She had made

Indian food, and the apartment smelled of curry and coconut milk. Terry and Rick arrived with an armful of gifts, and we gathered round to admire Peter's gigantic new home entertainment center. A projector with three colored lenses sat incongruously on the living room side of the kitchen counter, looking vaguely like one of my brother's hand made telescopes. It pointed toward a large pull-down movie screen.

Kari still smoked as readily as she laughed, which was often. "I've tried to quit, but every time, I gain more weight." She took her cigarettes outside, and never smoked around our kids. That year she had received a camera as a gift from Peter, and took two rolls of photos before dinner was even served.

Kari and Cedar were unlikely pals, their ten year age difference insignificant. Sometimes Kari got on her knees and Cedar rode her back like a pony, both of them screaming with laughter. Once they spent an entire weekend together making earrings for all their friends out of little drilled gemstones, quietly working side by side in the filtered white light of her apartment balcony.

Cedar's gift for Kari was a giant chocolate bar from Trader Joe's. She had wrapped it in gold foil but the heady fragrance reached Kari before she tore it off.

"Mmm, chocolate!" she laughed happily. Cedar's eyes glowed with pleasure. It was a sure thing, chocolate being Kari's weakness, especially the dark kind, which this was, of course.

I put on the black hat from Terry and long fringed scarf from Kari and posed in front of their fake fireplace. Terry and I had our arms around each other's shoulders and David stood smiling in the background, wearing his "Go A's" fan t-shirt, bought the year they won the World Series.

Terry gave Rick a pair of musician's gloves, with the fingertips cut out for playing music on the street. He was wearing them, complaining about the poor quality of today's winter wear. "See?" he said in mock exasperation, wiggling his bare fingertips. Paper and ribbon were piled in corners like the remains of a holiday parade as we sat with steaming plates of fragrant dhal and curry, spread out over the couch and floor.

"What a homecoming!" We said our goodbyes at midnight, the last to leave with the furthest to drive.

David and Cedar fell asleep on the way home. "It's so good to be back North, isn't it?" I grinned in the darkness until I fell asleep too, and Ed turned on the radio to keep himself company.

17

CITY MOUNTAINS

Ed and I wanted to live in the Santa Cruz Mountains, just above the city of Los Gatos. There were hundreds of properties for sale that had been damaged by the 1989 earthquake. Some of them had cracks in their foundations or had shifted off them completely, but even with these flaws most of them were completely out of our price range. A shack without running water or electricity was selling for over a hundred thousand dollars.

One house we went to check on was down a canyon road, and on that particular afternoon the area was in the middle of a ladybug invasion. Thousands of the insects had set up their winter headquarters there, perching on trees, flying into our windshield—and when we arrived, crawling around inside and outside of the little ranch house. I learned two things about ladybugs that day. They bite, (at least under those extraordinary conditions) and they stink, (at least to my human perception.) But they were not what scared us off from that place. The old man, who had bought his home in 1955 for eleven thousand was asking three hundred fifty thousand for it now.

That afternoon we took a break from house hunting and pulled off on a mountain road to stretch. Ed opened his door and on the ground, right in front of his left toe, was a snapshot of Jerry Garcia. Not a clipping from a magazine, a snapshot. He looked so friendly in the photograph that I thought it must have been taken by a friend. Ed stuck it in his pocket. "Maybe it'll bring us luck."

But after four months of looking, we gave up. The only one we had found in our price range was a Quonset hut. We might have afforded that one, but I couldn't picture even our unconventional family living in a long metal dome without windows.

We ended up in the Santa Cruz Mountains anyway.

Ed rented a little house from Robert and Sally who owned land off Summit Road. Deep in the trees, their property was high enough to see all the way to Capitola and the twinkling lights of Monterey Bay at night.

They owned three houses, all hand-built by the two of them with very little outside help, and all within twenty five yards of each other. Robert was in his fifties then, a little grizzled and pot-hazed. He had bought the land after a successful career as a businessman, having decided he would rather spend his days tinkering with old computer parts and elderly automobiles. He had at least fifteen of these in various stages of rust and decay parked in no particular order, like a miniature junkyard. Sally was a little younger, blond and attractive in a strong and outdoorsy way. She spoke with a hillbilly accent, but was sharp and full of interesting stories about past tenants. The house Robert and Sally lived in was at the edge of their property. It was made of old wood and scrounged tile and inside Sally had an aviary with zebra finches, canaries and a Peking robin. She kept her place full of plants because Robert was a chain smoker and the plants made the inside air tolerable.

There were some other interesting touches inside their house; a spiral wrought iron staircase in the middle of the floor that curved up to their tiny bedroom and a frog that lived somewhere inside, serenading them to sleep at night.

The big house, the one they counted on to make their mortgage payment, was beautiful but way out of our rental price range. They had built it with extra high ceilings and added a redwood deck on the same side as the floor to ceiling windows, which faced the woods. When we moved into the third house, the big one was still empty. The last family who lived in it had stiffed Robert and Sally out of months of rent then scuttled away in the middle of the night. They left a fluffy grey kitten behind that Sally adopted and named Loki, after the Norse god of mischief.

The place we rented was the smallest of the three houses. It was the top of a duplex, eight hundred square feet and only one bedroom with a door (David's). Ed and I slept upstairs in the loft, right underneath a little skylight with a square view of outer space at night. The only bathroom was upstairs, next to our room.

Cedar had a narrow room off the living room, really an indoor porch where her bed and dresser barely fit. She complained about not having a door but that room was definitely not designed for one. The entrance was wide with a tiled curve at the top.

The best part of the house was the stone fireplace with the wood-burning stove. It was our only source of heat but it kept that little place toasty in the winter. We had a cord of wood delivered in the fall and got our kindling down the road where a couple of barely tolerant dogs allowed us to pick up dry wood from the site of the new house being built.

It was here that Molly discovered a love of hunting, but she never ate what she (sometimes) killed. One night Cedar was awakened by a commotion. In the moonlight streaming in from the windows, Molly's shadow against the living room wall was gigantic. She was batting a beleaguered mouse through the air in a surrealistic dance of catch. Cedar was appalled and woke us up yelling for her to drop it.

Next door to the property was an old pear orchard where a plump brown and white pony lived. He got fatter every fall when the pears dropped on the ground and became accessible. On the same land were two miniature goats that butted heads and climbed whatever they could to see who could get the highest in their little barnyard. When Cedar and I went to get the mail from our box, we stopped to pet their bristly heads.

Cedar made friends with a black duck that lived in the pond Robert had made by digging out tons of dirt several years earlier. I have a photograph of her sitting on the bank with Mr. Duck climbing into her lap. Cedar's head is bent toward him, her long brown hair hiding most of his body, all but the orange bill. Mr. Duck was so loud we could hear his hearty quacking all the way inside our house with the door shut.

Cedar visited her friend daily, bringing him homemade bread scraps and corn she'd hold out for him to gobble from her palm. The duck would not let anyone else near him.

On a cloudy Saturday afternoon six months later he was missing. "Daddy, I can't find Mr. Duck!" She'd made her afternoon pilgrimage to the pond with a handful of cooked rice, planning to surprise him with this novel treat.

"Come on, I'll help you look." Ed and Cedar walked back to the pond hand in hand. They searched along the bank, Cedar calling his name, both of them plodding bravely through the muck.

Finally they discovered his limp feathered corpse on the opposite side, most likely a victim of the new neighbor's dogs.

Ed put him in a plastic bag and carried him back from the pond to our house with Cedar walking behind him, loudly and unashamedly sobbing. It was the first time Cedar had lost something so dear. After Ed buried him, she had a little remembrance ceremony above his backyard grave. We talked it over and decided he'd find a new duckling body in a safer pond, far from unpredictable mongrels.

One summer day Terry called and said she was coming for a visit the very next week, taking the train from San Francisco. Ed was in Las Vegas at an art show so Cedar and I met her at the station in San Jose, holding up signs that said *"Terry"* and staring straight ahead like we had no idea who she was. She laughed when she spotted us. "You guys," she said, shaking her head.

We drove home on the freeway and when I got too close to the dividing bumps Terry said I was "driving by Braille." She made terrified little noises when I swerved, then laughed at herself and apologized.

One of Robert and Sally's more spectacular creations was a large kidney shaped swimming pool completely lined with multi-hued blue tiles only an inch square each. When it was full of clean well water on a sunny day it was dazzling. David and Cedar spent warm mountain afternoons playing in the water and sometimes I joined them, sliding over the smooth blue tiles into that momentary shock of cold. The second best part was drying out on a lounge chair above the hot white concrete. I tried to get Terry to go swimming with us. "I never go swimming, anymore," she said. "I can't stand wearing a prosthetic breast."

Terry taught me how to make tempeh salad while she was there, and to this day I think of her when I add the mayonnaise and garlic and wonder what else it was she put in, because mine still doesn't taste quite right. I had her recipe for a while but lost it somewhere between 1992 and today.

Terry was lonely because Rick was in Russia, touring. She told me he was billed as "The Greatest Rock and Roll Player in the United States." He played to sold-out audiences and appeared on television shows in every town where he was booked.

"Rock and roll player?" I laughed. "Has he called you?"

"Yes, a couple times. He hasn't been able to tell me much, so I'll have to wait till he gets back to get the whole story." Terry was upstairs, looking at the little strings that were hanging from the ceiling above the railing. "What are these for?"

"It's my invention for rainy days. Our roof leaks in a million places and I direct the drips down the string and into buckets." She laughed, but it really worked—I wasn't kept awake by plopping sounds when the drips hit the bucket from several feet away. Robert's attempts to plug the holes in the roof with tar had failed every time.

Terry and I walked to the meadow. Peter was getting married soon, not to Kari but to someone he had met recently, right after they had split up. "Where do you think we should have the rehearsal dinner?" I asked her, looking down the grassy slope towards Capitola.

"You guys don't have to help out with that," she told me.

"Of course we will." I said. "So have you got a plan?"

"Well, I was thinking about the Chinese restaurant in Larkspur. It would hold all of us, even the out of town guests."

The wedding would be on a weekend in September, just a couple months away. Cedar was to be the flower girl, dressed in lace with a French braid and a crown of baby's breath circling the top of her head. The image of her leaving the salon like a medieval fairy would be the clearest image I would have of that day.

I took Terry to the train station on Sunday night. Rick was coming home that week and promised to bring her some painted Russian eggs. "Call me tomorrow!" We talked practically every day. Terry once said to me "We have to write a book together one of these days. No one would believe we were such dear friends unless they heard our whole story, and maybe not even then."

18

DANCE LESSONS

When Cedar was three years old, she taught herself to walk en pointe in her round-toed, pink athletic shoes. She could do this all the way across the linoleum floor in our Florida kitchen.

When she was six, she announced that when she grew up she would be a ballet dancer and move to France.

When she was eight years old she performed a solo dance on stage at a school event in Los Angeles, the star of the show. She wore a satin leotard in teal and danced free-form across the stage, smiling in my direction.

The school sold videos afterwards and I didn't buy one, shortsightedly thinking that I would never have a VCR and television. I tell myself, so I don't feel too terrible, that the tape would have deteriorated by now anyway.

After we moved to our home in the Santa Cruz Mountains we enrolled Cedar in one of Marie Stinnett's jazz dance classes in Campbell, her first lessons outside of school. Marie was in her late fifties then, an old pro who had been a dancer and extra in blockbuster films from the 1950s, like *It's Always Fair Weather* with Gene Kelly and *These Wilder Years* with James Cagney. She even appeared in *The Ten Commandments* with Charlton Heston. Marie had sent dozens, maybe hundreds of dancers off to professional careers over her teaching lifetime.

She was both tough and kind, a tall slim woman with the body and grace of a much younger dancer. She demonstrated pirouettes and relevés again and again in her large mirrored studio for Cedar's class of fellow nine-year-olds.

But Cedar's very first dance class with Marie was a disaster. I saw it building up during that hour. She had missed something, then couldn't follow what the other girls were doing, got frustrated and endured until it was over, fuming silently.

When I said goodnight to Marie, Cedar was quiet, a bad sign. Ed and David were waiting for us in the studio parking lot. Ed cheerfully asked "How'd it go?"

Cedar blurted out "Terrible!" then cried all the way home next to David who briefly tried to intervene.

"Cedar, I'm sure it's just because it was your first class."

"Shut up, David!" followed by renewed wailing.

We were used to Cedar's dramatics. When she had recently lost a board game, she stormed from the house, slamming the door and shouting, "It's not fair!" It took at least an hour for her to cool down.

"I'm never going back to dance class," she said bitterly as I tucked her in.

"I understand. Why don't we talk about it tomorrow?"

"Okay, but I'm not changing my mind."

Molly finally coaxed her to sleep, purring next to her ear.

I called Marie the next day and told her what happened. She thanked me and promised to write Cedar a note.

Two days later it arrived. "Look Cedar, you got a letter from your dance teacher." I handed it to her.

"Oh," she said dully. She took it to her room and sat reading it on the bed. After a few minutes, "Mommy, this is so *nice*!" she hopped up, beaming, and handed it to me.

The note was written in beautiful flowing script, inside a card with a Degas ballerina on the front. Marie said that she understood why Cedar might be upset, and how difficult it is to learn so many new things in one class period. *"Let me know if you'd like to give it another try, because I'll welcome you back, but I understand if you decide not to return."*

The next Thursday, Ed and David dropped Cedar and I at the dance studio, and then wandered down to the comic book and record shop a couple of blocks away. David had developed a connoisseur's taste for a specific artist in the super hero genre and spent that whole time looking for that artist's comics, which really were beautifully drawn.

Ed spent that hour looking through old blues albums, spending it flipping through dusty rows and discovering gems I would never have had the patience to weed out.

Because I've always felt awkward moving with intentional grace, I took enormous pleasure watching Cedar's dance class. When she mastered something she glowed for hours, practicing it at home that very night and working on it again before school the next morning.

After a couple of years at Marie's studio, she trained for the biennial "Dance at the Gym" extravaganza and took extra classes to get ready.

The night of the performance arrived. There were hundreds of people waiting to get seated on the hard bleachers (it really does happen at a gym) and I saw a woman, a plump, middle-aged stranger in line ahead of me wearing a pair of my pink clay pig earrings. Maybe a gift from someone who had bought them at an art fair? I decided against the pointlessness of introducing myself.

The three of us wormed our way onto some bleachers with a good view of the polished wooden floor where all the action was about to take place. It was hot and stuffy and I had butterflies in my stomach for Cedar. I always had butterflies before one of her performances. The funny thing was that she never got nervous herself, and I had to explain to her what that felt like. That night they had forty minutes to build up, little thrills surging through my gut while the youngest children danced and Cedar's group waited to go on.

They appeared at last, wearing ocean blue costumes decorated with little tinkling silver stars that I could barely hear when their steps carried them close to where we sat.

Cedar's movements were confident and graceful, and she turned her head to smile at us. The butterflies were replaced with a swelling in my chest, like an expanding heart.

We found her afterwards, flushed and happy, and I gave her the white carnations I'd held fragrantly close in my lap for the past three hours.

Not long after, we moved again, this time eighty miles northeast of Sacramento but Marie and Cedar corresponded for years. Marie followed her budding career through ballet, tap and theatre. Her letters, written in flowing cursive, were kept with Cedar's most valued treasures.

When Cedar died, I wrote to Marie and received this note back from her:

"Cedar will always have a very special place in my heart. We will be dancing together someday."

19

MOLLY

Whenever we bought film Cedar asked to borrow the camera so she could take pictures of Molly. We have dozens of photographs of the cat doing the same three things; lying upside down on Cedar's bed, sitting in the grass or lying upside down someplace else.

When Cedar was thirteen she wrote and illustrated *The Book of Molly*, and glued one of those photos on the cover. Molly is on her back, straddling a wooden stool with her two hind legs. Her head is half-way lifted with languid golden eyes looking right at the camera. Surrounding the title and marching all around the cover are little silver footprints drawn with a gel marker.

Every page has a drawing of Molly plus lofty thoughts about her possible origins. *"Is she really an Egyptian Princess?"* On this page Cedar's colored pencil rendering has Molly wearing a golden cobra with little blue beads dangling down on her striped forehead. The edging has a border of colorful hieroglyphs.

"Is she from Rome? Is that her sweet home?" A drawing of Molly standing in front of a building with columns dressed in a toga. Laurel wreaths decorate the top of the page. And so on. It's carefully crafted and bound in a clear notebook. On the back cover she wrote *"By Cedar Rosenfield, May 18, 1994."*

Molly slept with Cedar almost every night, crawling under the covers and *playing the piano* on her exposed flesh. Cedar told me about this one day when I asked why she had scratches on her legs. "Don't let her do that!" I was appalled.

"I don't want to disturb her," she told me.

Molly stayed close to home most of the time we lived in our little mountain place. A young couple had moved into the big house next door and they owned a large rottweiler-mix. Sometimes we'd find him on our front porch when we returned from an errand, growling menacingly when we tried to go inside. I knocked on our neighbor's door, "Your dog got out again."

"Oh Max," Sandy said under her breath, tramping across the short distance between our houses and yanking him home by the collar.

Sandy worked as a park naturalist and would occasionally bring us wild orange mushrooms she collected on her patrol. The kids thought they looked like alien brains but Sandy told me, "Just sauté them in a little butter." I did and they were delicious.

After she gave birth to a daughter, I brought Sandy a casserole. "This is a thinly veiled excuse to see the baby," I told her. She laughed and took me upstairs.

Makia was beautiful. She had lots of dark curly hair like her mama and was already fat with breast milk. I didn't pick her up but admired her sleeping in her bassinet with deep purpose, in the way of all newborns. The light from two walls of windows softened the entire scene, like a Mary Cassatt portrait. "What a beautiful baby," I said.

When I was leaving, Max sidled up to me. As I opened the door he lunged for the skin on my upper arm and nipped me. Sandy shouted "Max!" in her most authoritative voice. Sandy weighed just ninety pounds to Max's one hundred fifty, but he cowed and slunk away, head held low and stubby tail flattened in submission. I was out of breath and only bruised, but Sandy was mortified.

I worried about her baby after that, because I thought that dog was definitely psychotic.

A couple weeks later I realized I hadn't seen Max for days. I asked Sandy about him and she told me he had died from a brain tumor just a week after the nipping incident. I was relieved, like some evil cloud had vanished from the property.

Molly ventured outside more and spent afternoons dust bathing in front of our house. Once she followed Cedar and me all the way to the meadow behind the property, past all of Robert's broken down cars, through the old apple orchard trail and up to our favorite hilltop spot. She stayed with us the whole time, swishing her tail and lifting her nose to the passing breezes.

Cedar called her "my furry sister" and David called her "Miss Molly Muffincakes". They both loved her, but when two stray tabby kittens wandered onto the property the kids begged us to keep them, too.

The answer and I'm sure they expected it, was "No" but we let David keep them in his room till we could find them a home.

One evening Molly had settled down in the kitchen to her favorite canned food dinner when the kittens escaped from David's room, rounding the corner in a wild striped scramble. They headed straight for Molly's food dish and she flew backwards, choking on her food. I don't think she had any idea there were kittens behind that door.

The next weekend we drove them to Sausalito where Peter's veterinarian found them a home together. A year later we learned those bedraggled orphans had been adopted together and gotten fat and sleek. The kids missed them, but Molly was visibly more relaxed.

20

ƩTITCHEƩ

David and Cedar were playing catch one afternoon when she got beaned just below her left eye with the softball. It looked like a deep cut and I really fretted she would have a scar. At the time that was the worst thing I could imagine happening to her.

Ed drove her to an emergency clinic in Santa Cruz where a young East Indian doctor gave her a couple of stitches and assured Ed there wouldn't be a scar and she was right. After it completely healed there was a fine white line for about a year, and that eventually disappeared.

The doctor also mentioned that Cedar had a heart murmur, but that wasn't so uncommon and she would probably grow out of it. The doctor's words translated to me by Ed, the professional softener of heavy blows, were reassuring.

The already mortified David got a lecture about playing ball carefully with his sister and I daubed her wound with my general panacea, aloe vera.

To find out something wasn't working perfectly in that otherwise lovely growing young body held my attention for a week or so and then got absorbed by life.

21

OUR OWN PLACE

By 1993, I was fed up with renting. "We have to get that down payment money together," I complained. We were supposed to be having a *quiet* evening at home but our downstairs neighbor was playing a reggae number on his off-key electric guitar and the amp was cranked up full blast.

"I think you're right!" Ed laughed, but that music was actually painful to me and I wanted to cry.

By now Ed and I were working together on The Magic Zoo. We spent our weekdays driving toward promising looking business districts near San Jose, spying out door-to-door selling territory. We divided up the area. He walked one direction and I headed the other. But sometimes he waited for me in the car, reading or listening to the radio while I made my rounds. "You're much better at it; I'll just be the driver and cheerleader." Ed hated the aspect of cold calling.

"Do you think I enjoy it?" I glared at him as I shut the car door with my hip, arms loaded with boxes full of jewelry. It was a half-hearted battle—I'd been making money this way for years.

Two hours later, I melted back into the car. I ventured tentatively, "What if I called my customers and set up appointments for you to go by and see them?"

"Sure, we can give it a try."

The next morning I pulled out a stack of business cards for the Fremont area, made twenty calls and had the following day's itinerary set by noon. *Could it be this easy?*

"Hey Ed, I have twelve appointments for you tomorrow!"

"What? Oh, that's great."

"Great? It's fantastic! I can spend the whole day creating new designs!" This, obviously, was only part of the thrill. I skipped to the couch and planted a kiss on top of his balding head.

A year later the down payment money was finally collected. The four of us walked single file down a tree lined lane, searching for the perfect family conference spot. "How about here?" Ed pointed out a gentle slope, far from houses and the poison oak that flourished red and waxy practically everywhere in the Santa Cruz mountains. One by one we scootched down the leafy hillside heading towards an enormous flat stone shaded by bay trees. "This looks like an Indian grinding stone," Ed was looking at a hollow spot in the center where Native American women might've ground acorns centuries ago. Perfect oblong acorns were scattered all around us, food for squirrels and birds now.

Ed pulled out a notepad. "I have as many pages as we need for everybody to write down what kind of home they'd like to have."

"I want to have llamas," Cedar spoke up, reaching for the notebook. "And my own room. With a door," she looked at me pretending to be annoyed so I'd laugh. "And I need to be close enough to Marie's studio for dance."

David wrote *"1. Places to play my music"* David had recently bought a bright red electric guitar with money from his job, and was already writing his own songs. *"2. Animals, especially llamas."*

We all agreed our house would be in the country and would have a lot of windows and light and a big vegetable garden. Ed and I wanted a couple acres of land and a wood burning stove.

The problem was finding a home near San Jose that we could afford. Three years had passed since we had last looked and prices had gone the wrong way for us, straight up. Even further out, past Gilroy and near Salinas we'd found nothing.

My old singing partner Andy lived in Sacramento, about an hour and a half from the Sierra Foothills and three or four hours from us. He was a professional graphic artist now, living in a tiny 1920s dollhouse tucked away near downtown. It was a hip area with a Starbucks and a sushi restaurant just two blocks away. Ed and I had stopped by before setting up an art show in the downtown convention center.

There was a framed poster on his kitchen wall, just behind the table. Tall skinny Andy and shorter curvy Merry holding our instruments and smiling in a black and white sketch from 1974. A friend of mine, Lisa, had drawn it to advertise one of our gigs. I remembered sticking them up all over Wichita, especially at the college.

Andy and I had remained friends all those years, settling down in different parts of California and seeing each other occasionally. On this visit, we sat in his living room on black leather chairs. Colorful posters he had designed for his clients covered the walls and the latest Mac equipment gleamed in one corner.

Andy is an exceptionally tall man. When I've not seen him for a while I get surprised by this all over again. He is also delicate in a way; small boned with graceful hands. "Musician's hands," my mother would say.

It was originally Andy's idea that Ed and I should live in the Sierra Foothills. "My friend Nan lives in Nevada

City—I go up to visit her on the weekends sometimes. We look through her telescope, eat at local places and generally have a fabulous time. There's a real arts community and a lot of live music. I think it's perfect for your family."

When we had a free weekend the next month, Ed and I made the five hour drive from San Jose. We drove past Altamont Pass and the white wind turbines, beyond Sacramento and onto Highway 49 uphill through the pine trees to Nevada City.

We parked, then explored downtown, straining our calf muscles in unaccustomed ways on the sloping twisty streets. We passed an old assay office with ancient mining equipment placed for historical interest right next to the sidewalk.

I especially wanted to see The Nevada Theatre, a solid two-story structure planted here firmly and with purpose in 1865. "Look at that," I said to Ed breathlessly as we turned onto Broad Street and spotted it a block away.

I rubbed my hands across the tired red bricks and read about Mark Twain performing here over a hundred years ago. I pictured him strolling across the stage in a white suit, puffing on a cigar and saying outrageous things to his Victorian audience.

Nowadays Foothill Theatre Company produced their plays there. They had a good logo and professional looking promotional stuff that I picked up to show Cedar.

There were no McDonalds, no Burger Kings, and no Motel 6s. Andy had told me, and I believed him after that trip, that unless your corporate office was located in Nevada City, you couldn't do business there.

But there was a glass-blowing shop, several restaurants, bars and shops with clothing and local crafts. All the buildings were those tall skinny brick structures created in a century when all objects and especially downtown businesses were expected to last forever.

The air smelled clean and I could tell from my shallow, faster breathing that the altitude had changed. We got back in the car and drove around the outlying areas, just a few miles from this artistic community heart, and we found plenty of homes for sale in our price range. None of them looked alike and all had an acre or two of land separating them from their neighbors.

Driving home the next day I couldn't stop talking about moving there, but Ed knew he had to find the house on his own. Besides not wanting to leave the kids alone every weekend, I hated looking for houses. It made me uneasy trying to picture our private world in so many environments, one after the other, sometimes five or six in one day. What would I do with *this* room, where would my studio be, what color should I paint the bathroom, could you put a cat door in, etc. It wore me out.

David had graduated high school, and had a job working in Palo Alto for a company doing phone sales. He drove to work in the little white BMW he'd bought with his own money. "I still want to play music full-time," he assured us, and practiced on his new electric guitar every night.

Cedar was thirteen years old. We had taken her from private school because we couldn't afford to keep her there and save up for a down payment at the same time. For a while she attended the local public school in the mountains, just a mile from where we lived. The building sat in a pine tree clearing, and had the best parking lot for roller-skating on the weekends. I took her there one Sunday and sat on a brick wall, watching her zoom by on her new blue Christmas skates. "Come on, Mommy, skate with me!" I had a used pair but they hurt my feet.

"Maybe in a minute." I breathed deeply. The air was scoured clean by acres of oak and pine above San Jose's smog zone. *This I will miss.*

The public school itself seemed adequate enough until one of her teachers *insisted* she outline her stories before writing them. This may seem like a small thing, but it really upset Cedar. "Maybe you could write your story first and create an outline of it before you turn it in," I suggested.

"Oh, Mommy, that would be stupid. Besides I don't want to lie to the teacher."

It was exasperating. Finally I did some research on the local home schooling movement and decided to give that a try. "We'll be moving soon anyway," I told myself. After enrolling her, she had a loose curriculum to follow, and spent most of her time writing stories. Molly sat beside her on the bed where she worked quietly, scribbling words on yellow-lined legal pads for five or six hours a day.

She also worked on visual art, concentrating mostly on anatomy. With great concentration she studied her left hand, capturing its bones and muscles in fine pencil lines on her sketchpad.

From the library she checked out photography books and drew nudes; her first attempts were clumsy, charming oddities with limbs too long or bent at the wrong places. She eventually taught herself to see what was there, her delicate line drawings capturing nuanced expressions and musculature perfectly. I sent a pencil sketch she had done of actress Ethel Barrymore's face to my mother, who commented "Cedar does delicate work for one so young." From Grandma Kate, this was high praise.

I was asleep one Saturday night when Ed climbed the stairs to our loft, softly called my name and handing me a fragrant purple lilac cone. "I've found our house," he said quietly.

I sat up in bed, "Really?" Ed had been gone for a couple days, scouting around outside Grass Valley and Nevada City, in the countryside.

"It's perfect. We can all drive there tomorrow to see it. The owners are wonderful people and they're selling it themselves."

We piled in the car early to make the long drive by lunchtime. Cedar asked, "Is there a dance studio nearby?"

"We'll find one," Ed said, with more confidence than he could have possibly felt.

The house was three miles outside Grass Valley, in the "Great Republic of Rough and Ready," an eye blink of an old mining town, now nothing but an abandoned blacksmith's shop and a liquor store next to a Mexican restaurant. The town was named after Zachary Taylor, who is incidentally one of my ancestors and was known by the men who fought under him as "Old Rough and Ready."

Rough and Ready had seceded from the Union in 1850 as a protest against unfair tax laws. They even had their own Flag, as displayed on a T-shirt Ed purchased from the liquor store. But only three months after seceding, the townspeople became sentimental at the approach of Independence Day and voted themselves back in.

Our possible new home was down Rough and Ready Road off Rough and Ready Highway, which later on confused people trying to visit us. We told them "Just turn right at the veterinary clinic on Rough and Ready Highway," but unfortunately there were two veterinary clinics on that road, and if I forgot to tell them to turn at the *second* one they'd get lost.

In the middle of that springtime Sunday, vibrant green pastures and blooming blackberry tangles lined our way there.

"Here we are!" Ed pulled into the long gravel drive. Rocks crunched under our tires, a curiously satisfying sound. We parked in front of a pale yellow, blue-trimmed ranch house, faintly reminiscent of a mobile home. "It's a *manufactured* home," Ed read my mind. "Wait till you see the whole thing before you say anything." The front yard was an expanse of green; colorful irises bloomed on the perimeter and lilac bushes grew in a natural rock garden across the drive from the front door. There were two of them, white and purple on either side of two large granite boulders, deposits from the last ice age. A young but already twisty oak tree sprung from the center.

Rodney and Alice greeted us with hugs. They were Hare Krishnas, but looked more normal than we did. No shaved heads or salmon-colored robes, they were dressed in middle class slacks and crisp looking ironed shirts. Alice did have long hair, but handsome groomed Rodney would've looked at home in a big city bank. As a matter of fact, he sold insurance.

The kitchen was just to the left when we entered and was painted a bright sunflower orange-yellow. Alice had a colorful little shrine fixed up on the kitchen counter with a photograph of their guru. Incense spiced the air. "I've made a vegetarian lunch," she said, smiling. She served it on stainless steel dishes and cups - the kind they use in some Indian restaurants. It was delicious—naan bread, aloo gobi, spicy dhal and mango lassis.

They had two young children, polite kids, who watched us curiously. Rodney and Alice were moving to North Carolina to join an Ashram. He was tired of his daily commute to Sacramento.

After lunch we got the full home tour, which took about four and a half minutes. It was a straightforward house, one you'd never get lost in. The living room had a wood stove and looked out the back to another pile of granite boulders and more oak trees. There was a new redwood deck off to the side.

There were three bedrooms, all of them off the hallway with one tiny bathroom next to the kitchen. In two of the bedrooms there was an entire wall of built-in drawers and bookcases. "I really like that," I said to Ed, not knowing the drawers would swell in the rainy season, becoming nearly impossible to open.

The house didn't have a traditional air conditioner. It used something I had never heard of called a swamp cooler, located on the roof of the house. Rodney explained how it worked. "You just flip this switch on the kitchen wall and that turns on the water which damps down the pads inside the cooler. Then you flip this other switch that starts the internal fan that blows cool air inside, which gets pulled through the wet pads from the outside air." I thought it sounded Rube Goldberg-ish but Rodney swore it was efficient and cheap to run and cooled the entire house on ninety-plus degree summer days.

The water was from a well. "It's delicious and pure," Alice told us proudly and handed me a glass. But I was used to drinking distilled water and thought this had too much of an actual taste.

From the deck Rodney pointed out the garden plot, a twenty-by-twenty foot space he had fenced in to keep out deer. "I dug in turkey manure last fall but haven't had time to work it so all that rich soil is just waiting to be planted." I wondered if Ed mentioned to him how much I wanted a garden. In front of the plot, closer to the outbuildings on the east side was a cherry tree, fallen white blooms covering the ground underneath like big lacy snowflakes. "You have to cover the tree with a net once the cherries are ripe," Rodney told us. "Otherwise the birds get them all."

Halfway down the back of the property was a pump used to pull water from the ditch below for watering the garden. The ground sloped so steeply you couldn't see the man-made stream unless you walked most of the way down and to get there you had to slant your body backwards as a counter-balance. I watched Ed and David disappear behind the tall grass with Rodney.

Cedar and I walked to the front where four sentinel cedar trees stood at least fifty feet tall just behind the white fence lining the road. Someone, probably the local Pacific Gas and Electric had clipped them away from the electrical wires by removing great crescent shaped bites from the center of the foliage.

In the middle of the yard, two crooked plum trees bloomed pink and white like twisted wedding cake confections. Later Alice told us "The plums are delicious, but small. The kids loved eating them in the summer." I thought about our backyard in Mill Valley.

Next door lived Albert and Dorrie, grandparents who had taken over the raising of their neglectful son's two young children. They had five acres with a large flock of rheas, great gangly South American birds akin to the Ostrich. "What's that sound?" Cedar asked me. I listened and heard a nearly subsonic booming. Actually, I more felt it than heard it, in the center of my chest.

"I don't know, it's kind of creepy," I said to her.

Rodney had reappeared with Ed and David. "Tell me, what's that low booming sound we heard?" I asked.

"Oh, that's the rheas," he said simply, "It's how they talk to each other, I guess."

Rodney said there was someone else interested in the ranch, as he called it. Even though I know that's the oldest sales trick in the book, we fell for it because we wanted this beautiful property. We gave him a deposit on the spot.

It became ours slowly, transferring hands with signatures and paper over the next couple of months.

When the green grass turned gold by June's dry heat, we packed up our Santa Cruz mountain home and prepared for the drive to our new place, five hours away. For the four years we lived there I had to leave room in every beginning conversation for the inevitable laughter that followed my answer to the question "Where do you live?"

22

MOVING DAY

ally approached us, strolling confidently across the
gravel drive with a birdcage in her arms. "I brought
you a going away gift," she said, grinning, a little slyly, I
thought. She climbed the stairs and set the cage down on
our front porch. I stared at the crippled yellow canary. He
was missing some of his toes and held onto his perch
tenuously making me gasp involuntarily every time he
fluttered to keep his balance. I thanked Sally absently
because I was trying like mad to figure out how to give him
right back. "He's a wonderful singer," she told me as she
left.

I did not want a bird. I like to watch birds fly outside,
where they belong. Molly however was thrilled. She threw

herself at the cage instantly, knocking him to the floor. Perfect! I picked it up and walked back to Sally's house to explain, "Our cat would only terrorize the poor thing the whole way to Rough and Ready."

"Oh, I see." She reluctantly accepted back the bird she thought she'd finally gotten rid of. Sally raised and sold her canaries as a hobby, and this was one she didn't have the heart to euthanize.

"Hop in!" Ed watched our approach. "So have you got that, David? I'll make sure we don't get far ahead of you." Ed fastened his seat belt and David started his BMW.

"Don't worry, Dad. I'll be fine."

The fat pony looked up, chewing, as our little procession drove past.

"I still wish I could hold Molly," Cedar was looking at me as we merged with the traffic on Highway 17. "Do you think she'll be okay?" The cat was riding in the towed car again.

"Of course. She's probably enjoying herself," I doubted that, but knew she would survive.

David trailed right behind all the way past Sacramento, when he suddenly fell so far out of sight I couldn't spot him in the rearview mirror. *Where the hell was he?* I wasn't thrilled that he was driving by himself that whole way anyway and not being able to see him now made me twitchy. "Shouldn't we pull over and wait for him?"

"Don't be such a worry wart," Ed demanded, impossibly.

At last we lumbered up the gravel drive to our new home where we waited for David who showed up ten minutes later. He explained a little sheepishly "I was just obeying speed limit signs on Highway 49." We evidently had ignored them.

It was hot; the green grass of last April now looked and smelled like hay. The iris blooms had disappeared into crowded borders of flat green spears, and plums were ripening on both trees, yellow and purple like Alice had promised. We wouldn't see a drop of rain again until September.

That night we slept on sleeping bags on the living room floor after eating dinner at the only restaurant in Rough and Ready—mediocre Mexican food but plenty of it. It was just what we needed.

The next day I cleaned the house before we brought in our furniture. It still smelled of incense and opening the windows didn't help. There were dead ants in a freezer full of sticky melted ice cream and the kitchen cabinets were full of crumbs. "Thanks a lot, Alice," I muttered.

I felt righteous about my own house cleaning Karma which propelled my energetic, vengeful scrubbing.

We planned to paint all the rooms white. This would be simple and relatively fast, but Cedar wanted her room wall-papered. "Sweetie, it would be so much easier just to pick a pretty color," I reasoned.

But she was adamant. "Remember, you promised me I could decorate my room any way I wanted."

Ed and Cedar spent hours at three different paint stores pouring through very large books filled with hundreds of designs. After two days of drama and hopeless, "I'll never find a good one!" she did. It was lovely; a careless, watercolor design of large pastel flowers.

"Cedar, that really is beautiful," I said. Ed looked relieved.

Cedar used her allowance money to buy white ruffled curtains for both windows, and I commissioned an artist we knew to make her a quilt to match the wallpaper. From a slip of leftover paper, Jane gathered bits of cloth for an exact match in teensy flower prints. "I can trade half the cost for some jewelry," I proposed as we sat in her studio to work out the details. Jane was thrilled but I was pretty sure I had the best end of the deal.

A week later I picked up my jewelry cases and drove to Penn Valley, three miles away. There was a little shopping mall there with a video store, beauty parlor, a realty office and so forth. I updated my opening remarks, trying them out in the realtor's office first. "Hi, I just moved to the area. I'm an artist and I make jewelry. Would you like to take a look?"

The woman at the front desk looked amused. "Sure, let me see if anyone wants to come out and see." She phoned to the back. "There's a lady out here selling jewelry."

She paused, listening. "Oh, all right." She turned to me. "They're all busy now, sorry."

In the two weeks I'd not been working I'd reverted to my natural state, which despite all indications was not a door-to-door sales person. "I hate this," I whispered to myself, walking out the door.

The woman in the optometrist's office next door at least looked. "These are cute. Can you come back next Friday, when I get paid?" I took her card, but was pretty sure I'd lose it before then. I gave her mine.

Back in San Jose, the towns were attached like strands in an endless necklace— sparkling new strip malls, dozens of veterinary clinics, doctors' offices and beauty salons with hundreds of potential customers. If I reached a desolate selling spot, I'd just move down a few blocks. This technique eventually created a customer base of several hundred people who actually looked forward to our visits and always had their checkbooks and cash ready.

Ed and I realized it would be foolish to give up these hard-won customers. So I called and set appointments and Ed drove back to San Jose almost every week, camping out with friends and driving around to see the most loyal on a rotating schedule, once every six weeks.

We were getting accepted into better art shows, juried ones which meant you had to submit slides and allow a team of critics to decide if you were good enough or edgy enough to participate. Most of these were further away, from southern California to Arizona or Nevada. Through this patchwork of income sources we paid our bills.

One of Ed's relatives once told me he could hardly believe we made a living doing what we did. It may have been a veiled insult, but I didn't care. I was proud of my jewelry and of an entrepreneurial path that originated well before medieval market places even evolved. "We're just following a proud tradition," I had told him.

23

DAVID

David was seventeen. He had a job working at the K-mart in Grass Valley, where he wore a thin red polyester vest over a white shirt and spent eight hours a day stocking shelves. "What do you really want to do?" I asked him. I was still annoyed with the high school teacher who had discouraged him from a career as a writer.

"You should get a law degree," he had told David. Silently, I accused Roger, maybe unfairly, of undoing a lifetime's worth of my rallying around a career in the arts.

"I don't know what I want to do." He seemed chronically bored.

About that same time David pierced his left ear, cut his hair super short, bleached it blonde and then dyed it bright blue, rinsing the color through his bristly head with the hose on the side yard. He had asked me about it first. "Mom, do you mind if I dye my hair blue?" He looked at me with raised eyebrows, hopefully. I didn't mind, not even the trail of diluted blue water that trickled erratically through the gravel and stained the stones through the first couple weeks of the rainy season. David looked handsome no matter what he did to himself; he'd inherited my grandmother's cleft chin and Ed's dark skin and broad shouldered frame.

David told me about a new friend, a woman named Dartha whom he had met at a rock concert in Yuba City. "Is it someone you're interested in?" I asked him casually and he knew what I meant.

"No, we're just friends. She's older than I am." That didn't bother me. As far as I was concerned friends could be any age or gender.

I asked David to invite her for dinner. She arrived in black Goth attire and makeup, a plump woman in her early thirties.

I found her peculiarly disturbing, mostly because she had so little to say. *Is she being careful of blurting out the wrong thing? What would that be?*

"I've made spaghetti, nothing fancy. I was planning to make garlic bread but I'm out of butter," I added, distracted.

"Put olive oil with diced garlic on the bread. That should work," she suggested.

She was right. The garlic bread was delicious.

Dartha reminded me a little of Peter's old girlfriend Kari, but Kari was an extrovert and Dartha answered all my questions in five words or less. There was a slight physical resemblance and lack of responsibility that seemed familiar. Was that what attracted David? I was mystified.

"What kind of work do you do?" I asked at dinner.

"I don't have a job," she replied, reaching for the salad.

"What do you want to do?" I asked.

"Write," she said.

"Are you working on anything now?"

"No."

That was how it went. Cedar and I cleared the dinner dishes and I got out bowls to serve apple crisp. When I looked over the counter to ask Dartha if she wanted whipped cream, she was holding David's hand. I pretended not to notice.

When David left to drive her home, Cedar took Molly into her bedroom for company while she worked on a new story. I called Ed, who was in Las Vegas. "How was the show?" I asked him.

"So-so. Michael and I just had dinner at the casino buffet and now I'm stuffed up with terrible food."

"I'm sorry. When you get back I'll make you lots of brown rice and veggies."

"That sounds good, but I don't want to think about food right now." He made a moaning sound.

"There is something I have to talk to you about."

"What's that?"

"I invited David's new friend Dartha over for dinner tonight—you know David said they were just friends—but after dinner they were holding hands and giving each other 'looks.' And I found out she's in her thirties!"

"Oh, no."

"He just left to drive her home. Can you talk to him when he gets back?"

"I think you should, you're right there."

"I don't know what to say to him!"

Ed was collapsed in front of the TV in a motel room after a day on his feet selling my jewelry and this was surely not the evening he had looked forward to, but I persisted.

He said, "Look, our son is seventeen years old. Sexual relations with this woman would be considered statutory rape."

We both agreed David had to stop seeing Dartha. But he insisted I be the one to tell him. "Ed, this isn't a parental skill where I particularly shine." I glared at the receiver.

"It wouldn't make sense for me to tell him to break it off with someone I've never even met," he said. "Besides, you'll do fine." I don't remember if I hung up without saying goodbye, but that impulse was definitely there.

When I heard David's wheels crunch on the gravel, I gritted my teeth and looked toward the ceiling. He was taking a long time to come in. After five minutes the knob turned and I pulled the door open. "David, let's go to the living room, we need to talk."

"Fine," he said dully, expecting the worst. We sat across from each other on two couches, sinking into the fat grey cushions.

"It looks like your relationship with Dartha is more than 'just friends,' am I right?"

He looked sheepish, but admitted that was true. I sat up straight, "Honey, this isn't right. She's seventeen years older than you!"

My kids had been raised to think for themselves, not necessarily based on staid middle class ideas. At this moment it came back to haunt me when he said "What difference does age make? We really like each other and I don't think that should be any kind of consideration, especially since it doesn't bother *us*."

What I was thinking and not saying was there was something creepy about a thirty-something woman interested in a high school aged boy, especially an innocent one like David. No drugs, no alcohol and a poetic soul besides.

"I just talked to your dad and both of us think you should cool it with Dartha until he gets home."

"I don't think you and Dad should be deciding who my friends are."

This conversation felt just like crossing a stream on a rolling log. My clumsy objections weren't matching David's native common sense and while he stood steadily I was about to fall off and drown. The worst part was knowing I was right.

I tried again. "I'm sorry, but you are still a minor, living at home, and if Dartha had sexual relations with you…" I stopped and looked at David quizzically.

"No mom, we have not had sex." He was disgusted.

"Anyway, it would be considered statutory rape," I concluded.

He was silent a long time, my words hanging in the air like an obscenity. Finally "Okay, Mom, fine." David was furious with me but he saw there would be no budging. "I won't spend time with her until Dad gets home but I have to see her in person to explain what's going on." I agreed to this warily, but was still relieved. The feeling was like yanking my child from the path of a barreling semi-truck.

Three days later Ed had returned and the four of us (Cedar was willingly in her room during this excruciating exchange) sat in the living room.

I asked Dartha pointed questions about her intentions toward David and what she thought about marriage. "I don't believe in it," she told me, glaring.

I informed her she could not under any circumstances have sexual relations with our son, because it was illegal and we would press charges against her if she did. David looked horrified. "I'm sorry to be so blunt but this is how we feel."

"Dad?" David's voice lilted with desperation when he looked at Ed, who took a few seconds to answer.

"Your mom is right. Maybe I would have put it another way, but I agree with her."

Dartha argued "Your son and I really like each other. Why is it any of your business what we do?" God, this woman was dense.

"It's our business because he's our son and we love him."

"Are you ready to leave?" David was hurt and humiliated by the two people he trusted most. He left to drive her home, and I was scared to death he wouldn't come back.

Ed and I knew the heart of the trouble wasn't Dartha. For months we'd been disturbed by David's general lack of purpose. "Are you interested in college?" I'd asked him more than once.

"Nah..." He probably could have gotten a scholarship, but it wasn't something I particularly steered him toward. I thought he should have a passion, and didn't care if he followed a formal route or something self-devised.

When David was back in his room, silent and fuming but safe, Ed and I talked about the future. He said "Maybe we should send him to L.A. to get sorted out." It was late but we were wide-awake and still worried. One of the Scientology centers in Los Angeles was geared toward helping newer members handle difficulties through various classes, offering professional guidance in ethics and Scientology counseling.

"Maybe it would be easier for him to figure out his life if he weren't living at home," I told Ed. "Sort of get a look from a distance."

"I think you're right."

By the time David got up the next morning I'd already gone over how to present this idea ten times in my mind but Ed told me "We'll just talk to him. Don't worry about it."

"Good morning," I looked up at David when he emerged from the bathroom scruffy headed and bleary-eyed. "Did you get some sleep?"

"Yeah."

"How about some pancakes?"

"Sure."

Cedar was still asleep, but the batter I whipped up could've fed a family of twelve. David sat across from Ed, staring intently outside.

"How are you doing?" Ed asked.

"Fine."

"David, look at me." His gaze swiped Ed's face quickly before sprinting back to the plum trees, which had become strangely fascinating.

"I'd like to talk to you about something."

"What?" His voice held an edge of belligerence. David wasn't a difficult teenager so this was a whole new dimension.

"Do you still have some attention on yesterday?"

"I don't know."

"Maybe you guys could take a walk while I finish making the pancakes." I didn't think an extra pair of listening ears was helping.

"Good idea. Come on David, let's go outside."

He followed his father disconsolately out the door. I watched from the kitchen window as they sauntered toward the road in their identical gait. David was listening to his dad. I imagined Ed's reasoning voice, logical and comforting.

Stacks of pancakes were warming in the oven when Cedar appeared. "Hi Mom, where is everybody?"

"Ed's talking to David outside. Would you like some pancakes?" We sat at the table, pouring maple syrup and spooning yogurt over our breakfast.

"How did it go last night?" she asked.

"It was tough, but we're getting things sorted out."

David and Ed came inside, still talking but congenially now. David actually looked relieved. "What's happening?" I asked.

"David thinks going to L.A. for a few weeks might be a good idea," Ed said noncommittally.

"L.A.? Why?" Cedar wasn't yet in the loop.

I poked her under the table, whispering, "I'll tell you later."

Two days later Ed and I drove him to the airport in Sacramento. David wept all the way but still hugged us before he got on the plane. "He's not over her yet, that's for sure. I feel so mean."

"He'll be fine." Ed squeezed my hand.

David called the next day, still bereft. "Sweetie, hang in there. Things are bound to get better."

"Yeah, I guess," he said without enthusiasm.

"I'll be glad when David really gets going. He's still upset." I'd hung up and found Ed in the bedroom, putting new strings on his guitar.

"I think we should take our attention off David, so let me finish this and we'll all go swimming."

We changed into suits, gathered our oldest bath towels, and drove down the hill toward the Yuba River. The parking lot was nearly empty. We slid down a short dirt trail to a path lined with fig trees and tall grass. This was late summer, and the fruit was ripe. "Mmm, these are delicious," Cedar was munching on a fat brown semi-globe she'd picked off a low branch.

"We might be the only people who eat them," I said.

The swimming hole was quiet. This was the middle of the week and the only other people, a young couple, were smooching on the big rock in the middle of the natural pool. Ed and I sat on the bank while Cedar dove in. "C'mon, it's not *that* cold!" She was laughing at us but I dreaded that first numbing shock. The water was runoff from mountain snow only barely warmed after a summer of sun.

"Mom, once you start swimming, it's fine. Come on!" She was getting a little testy.

"Okay!" I plunged in, gasping involuntarily. *Only for Cedar*, I thought. Ed stayed where he was. I doggie paddled to her and noticed her teeth were chattering.

"Let's race to the other side!" I said, but of course she got there first and laughed at my stately approach. I could barely swim—and never fast.

Ed finally dipped in his toe and decided it was too cold, but Cedar and I swam and splashed for another half hour.

The next morning David called. "I had a session with Mark yesterday, and then read some things that are making a lot of sense." His voice sounded much brighter. "Mom, thank you and Dad for sending me here." I plopped into a chair, grinning with relief.

Six days later he called again, and this time his entire space was incandescent, the miles between us lit up and shortened. "Mom, I need to tell you something."

"Sure, what's up?"

"I've decided to join staff at the church here in LA."

Silence on my end, processing this. "Mom, did you hear me?"

"Oh, yes, of course. I'm just a little surprised." To my horror, I was getting weepy.

"Mom, what's wrong?"

"Oh, David, I never thought you wouldn't be coming home. Are you sure this is what *you* want?"

"Yes, Mom, this was totally my decision." He explained he'd be working in a branch overseeing the success of other Scientology organizations around the country, a position of some responsibility.

I knew I should be supportive and proud but instead I broke down and bawled. "Mom, tell me what's going on!" he was worried.

"It's just a surprise. I'm sorry, honey. It'll take me a little while to get used to this. Of course I'm happy for you," but I really wasn't yet.

"I'll be home soon to pick up my stuff and I'll be with you for a week. After that I'll have vacations and holidays at home, two weeks every year. Besides, you can come and visit me anytime you want."

Just four hundred miles away, I thought.

I gave the phone to Ed and sat on the couch, wiping tears.

"What's going on?" Cedar asked me, worried. She'd been in the living room the whole time, petting Molly and listening to my end of the conversation.

"David joined staff in L.A."

"But that's good, isn't it? He'll make new friends, and have a better job. Plus, no Dartha," she added smiling slyly.

"That's true," I said and gave her a hug.

It was time to put attention on Cedar's upcoming school term. She was entering the middle school years and I'd heard about a charter school program being organized in the area. Ed and I went to the first meeting where there were a surprising number of other parents interested in the same sort of thing. Perfect, and in the nick of time—it all came together with a building, teachers and a curriculum heavy with music and art.

David came home for a week, packed his room and actually cleaned it before he left. He didn't have a lot of stuff to take with him, his red electric guitar and a suitcase full of shorts and t-shirts. He would wear a uniform at work. I hugged him and kissed him goodbye, but found that I couldn't go with them to the airport. I was still a little tender about the whole thing.

24

BRACES

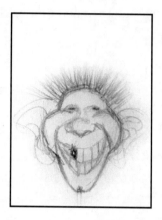

Poor Cedar had inherited my crooked front teeth. I thought her overbite was scarcely noticeable, a much less dramatic version of my own but she promised me it would be a definite liability to her as a performer. "OK, we'll talk to some orthodontists and see what they have to say." I set the first appointment with someone down the hill from Rough and Ready in the town of Auburn. The receptionist there had bought jewelry from me earlier that year. "It's a place to start," I told myself.

The waiting room had aqua plastic chairs, new in the 1960s, and a high window to prevent either escape or dreaming. We were too nervous to flip through the outdated magazines. "My niece loved the cow necklace!" Christina peered around the corner of her office, smiling.

"So this is your daughter!" Dr. K. filled up the doorway. He was a tall man with glasses, curly hair sprouting carelessly on either side of a balding dome.

"Come on back and let's take a look." I followed them to an examining room and Cedar settled back on a cracked leather chair. She folded her hands over her stomach, mouth wide open to his probing.

He was silent during the exam but afterwards made a fantastically insensitive remark, "You know, beauty is only skin deep." *What an idiot*, I thought about him and myself too, for bringing her here. Cedar was as gawky a teenager as she'd ever be, annoyed by acne, unruly hair and the whole reason we'd come.

When we got home, I flipped through the yellow pages. Dr. M.'s office was in downtown Grass Valley, just ten minutes away. *He can't be any worse*, I told myself as I dialed the number to make an appointment.

A few days later we parked under an exuberantly florescent orange-topped maple growing right in the middle of his asphalt parking lot. "Look how beautiful!" I pointed it out to Cedar, who looked a little worried about her immediate future. "Maybe it's a good sign," I told her.

Dr. M. was a small, quiet man with a neatly trimmed beard. He examined Cedar gently and recommended treatment. Braces for eighteen months and head gear for a year (day and night) of that time. He could start with her as soon as the first payment was made, sometime next week.

"Would you like a free evaluation as well?" He was so kind that I didn't mind what that obviously implied. *Well, he is an orthodontist*, I told myself. But my prognosis was complex. To have perfectly straight front teeth I'd need *jaw surgery* to correct my overbite.

"Would you do the surgery?" I asked him.

"No, but there is someone I can recommend."

I read the literature he handed me and thought about it for a few days. *A perfect smile*, I thought dreamily. But the prospect of major surgery, fifteen thousand dollars, and the possibility of failure turned me from it.

Also, "Forget it! I love you how you are!" from Ed, the only person who tells me I'm beautiful on a regular basis.

Cedar was fitted for braces the next week. "How are you doing?" I asked her on the way home.

"It feels weird and tight in my mouth. Do you think I could have some ice cream?"

"Would that help?" I was grinning.

"I'm sure it would."

The adjustment to head gear was harder. This was an awkward looking metal contraption that attached to Cedar's braces with a plastic strip that went all the way around the back of her head. Out in public, she believed people thought she was retarded or had some kind of congenital handicap. In the parking lot of our supermarket when a young child pointed at her curiously and said loudly to his mom "Look at that girl with the weird thing on her face!" Cedar glared at them ferociously.

The following July Cedar and I traveled to The Gilroy Garlic Festival, one of the larger food-themed art shows in California. We were on our own for a day before Ed joined us, but back then I could set up the entire booth easily enough. There were no heavy glass cases and all my jewelry hung on light-weight cloths or sat on a folding table. The show actually started the next day, so after organizing the inside we zipped up the heavy plastic tent and got ready to leave for our hotel.

"Hold on," Cedar told me, before unzipping the tent and walking back inside. I could tell she was in the midst of a "Little Nerd" moment of inspiration.

Years earlier David had invented the Nerd character. "Hello, my name is Egbert Squigg," he'd say in a purposely annoying nasal tone that made us all laugh. When he moved to L.A., Cedar invented a female version. She became "The Little Nerd" and I had to be "The Little Nerd's Mother." When we were in character we were deeply suspicious of each other's intentions, casting unfriendly looks back and forth and sneering unpleasantly. It was live theatre invented for our own amusement.

"Cedar, what are you doing?" I was exhausted and ready to flop on a hotel bed, in no mood for "Little Nerd" hijinks.

But Cedar was zipping the front flap up from the inside, leaving a small space near the top. I heard her climbing up on the stool.

Suddenly her head popped out through the opening.

Eyes squinting with malice, the disembodied head snarled at me, "We aren't open yet. What do you want?" I doubled over with laughter; Cedar had incorporated her head gear to enhance the overall effect of this thoroughly unpleasant character.

On the day Cedar finally had her braces removed, I drove her to Dr. M.'s clinic a little early. Claudia, the receptionist had her camera out. It was a tradition to take a picture of the smiling, braceless patient next to Dr. M., and tack it up on the bulletin board in the waiting area. Cedar grinned at me and walked through the doors to the treatment area for the last time.

When she reappeared forty-five minutes later, her mouth was pointedly closed. "Let me see your smile!" I blustered happily.

She shook her head "no" and went outside to wait for me in the car while I paid the final installment. No scene in the office was the idea, but I was sure there would be one in the car. It was mystifying.

"What's wrong?" I asked her as I climbed into the car. She was hunched against the door.

"My teeth are too big!" she yelled, infuriated with this disappointing outcome.   "Let me see," I demanded.

She opened her mouth in a mirthless grin and I realized at that moment she'd gotten so used to her braces taking up room that she'd forgotten what an *unpaned* tooth looked like. Picture windows, after all look so much bigger than the other kind.

"Cedar, your teeth are beautiful!"

"Yeah, right. They are gigantic!"

She moped for a couple more days until her perspective settled down. Being entertained by how slick her teeth felt without all that metal covering them when she glided her tongue over the unimpaired surface helped.

By the time Ed returned from our latest art show a week later, she wore her bright straight smile without a whit of concern. "I thought you told me she was upset about her teeth," Ed said later that night.

"She *was*. But you know Cedar."

25

AUGUSTA

I hadn't found a dance studio for Cedar yet, but we visited every one within a twenty-five mile radius, starting with a seedy little Grass Valley tap-dance studio. We spent a painful hour there, carefully not looking at each other, while menopausal women tapped in a graceless line, hands on the hips of the one in front of her to *I Wish They All Could be California Girls*. Afterwards, we dashed to the car to relieve ourselves of pressurized mirth, leaking tears of laughter and rubbing our traumatized stomach muscles.

An ad appeared in our new phone book *"Professional Ballet Lessons Taught by a Former Member of the Royal Ballet."*

"Cedar, look at this!" I called the phone number and spoke to a woman with an upper class British accent. *So far, so good.*

"Yes, you may sit in on a lesson this Thursday at two o'clock."

We drove thirty miles and parked across from the studio, which was in the upstairs of a tired looking office building in the downtown area of Auburn. There was a consignment store directly across the street and a rental office on the ground floor. The building was half occupied, dark and cheerless.

We rode the elevator with two quiet girls wearing ponytails and leotards. "Do you like your ballet lessons?" I asked them.

"They're hard," one of them replied.

Good, I thought.

The room where Augusta taught was a huge empty space, lined with ceiling to floor mirrors and barres along two walls. Young girls were arriving, sitting quietly on the floor or doing some preliminary warm-up exercises in front of the mirrors. A small wiry woman with short-cropped hair saw us and approached. For some unknown reason she was wearing heavy stage makeup "You must be Mrs. Rosenfield. And this is Cedar." She introduced herself, shook our hands and told us we were welcome to stay the entire hour, motioning us to some folding chairs along one of the walls.

"Thank you," I replied, smiling.

She put a Chopin piece on the record player. The children lined up in two rows, quietly and with all their attention focused on Augusta, whom I immediately realized with delight, was the real thing.

Augusta was a tough teacher. I was exhausted for the students and by the end of the hour was hoping Cedar could keep up with this class. She'd never had ballet lessons, as Marie's school was primarily jazz-oriented. I told this to Augusta but she was unfazed and signed Cedar up for the following Thursday, giving us a list of what we'd need to have by then—her first soft-pink, leather ballet shoes and a matching leotard and tights.

The following week we were back. Cedar's hair was pulled back in a long ponytail and she wore the official pink uniform of a young ballet student. I thought she was beautiful. "Do you want me to stay?"

"I don't care," was her slightly testy reply, which meant I'd better.

Since classical jazz has a lot of ballet components, Cedar was able to follow along pretty well. I kept my eyes on her and thought she did fine, but she didn't look happy. Augusta was a tough bird, barking corrections, seeming a little annoyed when things weren't perfect. *Oh no*, I thought.

The hour was over and Cedar looked at me witheringly as we left the studio. "What did you think?" I asked her. We were in the car now, driving up the long hill towards home.

"She's mean."

"Yes, but she also knows what she's doing. And she's the best we've found in this area."

Cedar sighed. That was all true.

She continued weekly lessons at Augusta's studio and later wrote a short script based on her experiences. This was intended to be a silent film, reminiscent of a 1920s comedy. She titled it, *A Little Discipline*.

Here are some excerpts:

"The film opens with a shot of a very large and regal looking building. In front of this edifice is a large sign, which reads The Gladys Hogwood Institute of the Arts. *The camera moves in to a close-up of the sign and then we fade to a shot of inside the institution.*

"It is a group of girls getting ready for ballet class. They look like a typical class, dressed in matching leotards and looking quite graceful. They seem to be in good cheer as they go about their business- stretching, etc. A few of the girls are en pointe.

"The soft piano music used to open the scene suddenly turns to a military march as we hear a drum roll and the door to the room opens. The instructress or 'general' appears in the doorway dressed in a coat, which might as

well be worn by an officer in the army. She is followed close behind by her assistant. The screen reads, 'The instructress—just a bit touched in the head.'

"The camera then cuts to close-ups of them both. The general has on a ridiculous amount of eye makeup- the kind used in ballet performances, only more so. She looks truly frightening. She flashes nasty looks at her pupils. Her 'aide-de-camp' helps her with her coat as she pauses dramatically by the door. However, her composure is shattered as he struggles with it, not knowing she has it tied in the front. Finally it slips down to the floor in a crumpled mess. She steps on it, gives him a hearty slap for his efforts, and pulls herself together after the less than dramatic entrance. The girls salute her, and she shouts, 'Forward March!' and herds them into the studio like a flock of geese with her stick. One last little girl makes a dash to get in with the others and the general slaps her in the butt with her stick then closes the studio door. The big clock on the studio wall reads 5:00.

"We fade from this shot of a clock to another, the one outside of the institute. This one also reads 5:00. Directly below this huge clock is a girl pacing back and forth looking at her watch, which reads 4:20. She yawns, stretches, and looks about her in a bored fashion. She has obviously been here for some time. She is waiting for class to start at 5:00.

"She wanders over to a bench and sits down, relaxing. She looks at her watch again, the camera shows that it still *reads the same and she, of course, doesn't catch on. She sits on the bench, doing mindless little things out of boredom and looks at her watch again, then puts her hands behind her head. Suddenly she sits up straight and looks at her watch. She puts it up to her ear, and of course it's not ticking at all! She gulps and looks at the camera.*

"*She walks out into the street, carrying her watch and looks up at the huge clock.* 'Late Again!' *reads the screen.*

"*Dropping her worthless watch in the street, she dashes for the door of the institute, slamming it behind her. The screen reads* '10 floors later'. *The girl is still running at top speed. She runs up several more flights of stairs when she suddenly stops, looks where she is and panics, for she's gone too far. She slides down the banister, has gone too far again, dashes back up a flight of stairs and disappears down the hall.*"

Once Cedar's heroine finally makes it outside the door (she's wearing a conspicuous leotard with stripes down the front), she hears "the general" speaking to the class:

"'*Ballet is no business for the weakling...The enemy is everywhere! You must be strong! Let nothing bowl you over!*'

"*On* 'let nothing bowl you over' *the instructress walks over to the side of the room where her assistant is standing in front of the door, just as the late* 'rebel' *manages to get the door open. The rebel flings the assistant on top of the instructress. The two are both* 'bowled over' *in one big lump as the girl sticks her head around the door. She makes a dash for her spot at the barre and is just in time for the* 'Inspection of the Ranks' *as the screen reads.*

"All is well as she looks at everyone with the most careful attention to detail. Then she comes to the girl. The screen reads 'A Rebel'. *There is a close-up of the girl's spiteful face as she looks at the general. The general sees the rebel's striped leotard and is too shocked and angry to say a word. Her face gets bright red and she says* 'Idiot! Where is your uniform?' *The rebel shrugs coolly and this breaks the general. She grabs one of the straps of her leotard, stretches it farther than it could possibly be stretched (everyone covers her eyes, including the rebel) and lets got of it. However, she's left her own hand on the rebel's bare shoulder and instead of the strap hitting the girl, the leotard snaps back on the general's hand. She hops away in pain and the rebel smiles, puts her hand out to lean on the wall and falls partly though a low open window which is there instead. The scene fades.*

"'Atten-shun!' reads the screen. Simultaneously every girl jumps into first position, their heels coming together at precisely the same time. After they are given the exercise, the girls begin, and the music they dance to is a classical adaptation of You're in the Army Now.*"*

Cedar's script continued with further embarrassments perpetrated on the general by our heroine. This is the grand finale:

"And the tables begin to turn. The scene opens with the rebel ranting about at the general. The general has a black

eye and is trying to escape her pupil. Finally, the rebel takes the general, boots her out the door with her foot and follows her into the hall, where we also find her assistant. 'Now, get!' reads the screen. And the rebel chases a little ways after them, clapping her hands at them like wild animals. 'Go on, get!' She claps some more and they disappear down the hall.

"The rebel is proud and still a little huffy. She struts into the studio and closes the door. She stands before the others, who are anxious to know what happened. Proudly, and in somewhat a mockery of the general, the rebel tells them 'Class is dismissed.' All of them cheer wildly. The rebel bows before them many times. Their celebration continues.

"The largest girls in the class pick the rebel up and lift her high in the air as they make for the door. The scene fades as the rebel collides with the top of the doorway."

26

OLD FILMS

Sometime during the month of our twentieth wedding anniversary, Ed and I decided to drive to Wilbur Hot Springs in Colusa County for the weekend. We hadn't been there since we had lived in Mill Valley and Terry watched the kids for us on a romantic weekend many springs earlier.

The great dancer Gene Kelly died that year, the day after our twentieth anniversary which was February 1, 1996. This led to the three of us watching *Singing in the Rain* at the independently owned Magic Theatre in Nevada City. And this became a turning point of aesthetic importance for our daughter. "That was brilliant!" she was smiling widely as we left the theatre, still reliving parts of the movie. "Gene Kelly's dancing was unbelievable! And that part where

Donald O'Connor danced with the dummy ..." her voice dissolved into laughter, purposely uncontrolled.

That's when I got the idea to buy a TV and a VCR. "There are so many classic movies she'd love to see... it'd be heaven for her."

Ed was noncommittal. "We'll see."

Cedar lobbied Ed for days. "It'll be educational, Dad. I can learn so much about early movie making."

We finally wore him down. At a TV repair shop Ed paid fifteen dollars for a used set and the owner threw in the VCR for an additional five bucks. But money wasn't the problem. We'd never had that blank moronic screen in any of our homes and Ed and I were both a little touchy on the subject. The promise of using it for movie-watching *only* solved this moral dilemma.

We rented *Philadelphia Story* with Katharine Hepburn, Buster Keaton's silent classic, *The General*, Charlie Chaplin's *Gold Rush*, and about fifteen others, all from different video stores within a five-mile radius. We practiced inserting the tape into the machine and made sure Cedar understood how everything worked. "Mom, it's really easy. I get it. You can even leave a little early if you want to." She had a refrigerator full of her favorite food and more films than she could watch in the two days we'd be soaking in the hot springs.

The next morning Cedar had the distracted look of a *project* in her eyes. "Don't worry about me, and have fun!" She waved us off from the front step.

Our route took us along Highway 20, into the flat green farmlands of early spring and up into the mountain air and land of Colusa County.

We stayed in the rustic Victorian Hotel right on the premises in a tiny wood paneled room with soft solar lighting and a shared bathroom that I would be bothered by anywhere else.

Strangers became friends for a couple days. We chopped vegetables side by side on the butcher block table in the large hotel kitchen and sautéed them in cast iron pots on one of two enormous gas stoves. My idea of a vacation did not involve having to cook, so we had brought pre-made Chinese dumplings from Trader Joe's to serve alongside the broccoli. It was pleasantly chummy, just one other couple sharing the kitchen facilities that first night.

We took our small feast into the dining area, sat at a candlelit table and ate. For dessert, we opened a dark chocolate candy bar, and let the sweet bitterness melt slowly on our tongues.

When we stepped outside, the velvety February night was crisp and starry. "Let's get into the water."

The springs, pool and sauna were clothing optional, but I never saw anyone wear a bathing suit there. All those different body types, fat, skinny, in or out of shape, male or female made no difference. We were all there for the quiet hills and the heavenly soaking.

Going from chilly mountain air to the perfect hot bathtub temperature all the way up to my neck, gently and persistently drew out every hidden shiver. I could feel them leave, like little electrical impulses disappearing into the surrounding mineral water.

After that first soak, I dressed and called Cedar, interrupting *Philadelphia Story.* "Kathryn Hepburn is an amazing actress! I *love* her! I can't wait for you and Dad to watch this movie."

When we returned on Sunday night, Cedar was in front of the television with a plate of French fries, watching Buster Keaton being pursued by the Union army. "Mom, Dad, you have to see this!" was how she greeted us.

Every Friday night after that weekend Cedar and I stopped at one of the four video stores in the area to collect our weekend quota of old films to watch. She had an uncanny way of knowing what would be entertaining just by reading the title and looking at the cover. Just because it was old didn't mean the movie would be any good, I discovered. But most of them were.

Oliver Hardy and Stan Laurel made her laugh so hard she'd grab her stomach and fall over sideways on the couch. In her favorite of their films, *Way Out West,* the two of them do a comedic pas de deux performed with surprising grace to a soft western song performed by a quartet of cowboys. It's unbearably funny and very dear. "How can two men be so *cute*?' she asked me rhetorically. Cedar could do a perfect impersonation of Stanley, especially when she'd just gotten up in the morning and could draw her freshly cut, short hair high with her left hand, smiling that wide and brainless grin.

Dozens of old stars were newly appreciated and given fresh life by Cedar's laughter. I wished Charlie Chaplin and Buster Keaton could know about the joy they brought our daughter, here at the very end of the century they had ushered in as silent clowns.

27

THE NUTCRACKER SUITE

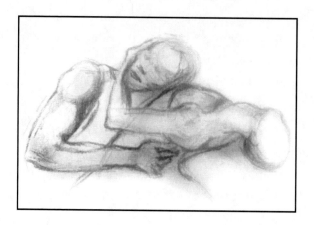

Augusta had been offered a position teaching dance at a university in the Southeast. She was aging and worried about life as an older artist without health insurance, so she took the job.

"There's an excellent dance school in Sacramento. It's associated with the Sacramento Ballet and I think Cedar would do very well there," she told us kindly. It was about eighty miles from Rough and Ready.

The school was near downtown in an older neighborhood with huge trees and well kept lawns, every house unique, built long before the days of developments and gated communities.

It was in a tiny strip mall sharing the row with a bakery and a used record store. We parked on a shaded side street with free parking.

The establishment was small, but there were at least three classes going on at the same time, each in one of three small studios separated by stucco walls. It was run by a woman in her seventies, a retired professional dancer and her daughter and son-in-law, also professional dancers from San Francisco.

For the first lesson Cedar was with the little kids so the instructor could get a sense of her training level. "Mom, this is humiliating!" she was insulted. But it was a testament to Augusta's professionalism that Cedar joined her own age group the following week.

I could watch if I wanted through a square glass window in the hall, and for months that's what I did. It didn't embarrass Cedar but I don't know why not. I must have looked funny from inside the studio. No one seemed to notice but Cedar, who occasionally glanced up and smiled.

After a couple of months the suggestion was made that we add more classes for Cedar. Since she'd started ballet late she needed more work to catch up with her peers, now en pointe.

It was expensive and I dreaded making that drive twice more weekly but I knew it was the right thing, and Cedar was dying to dance en pointe. I agreed, adding a Saturday and mid-week class. That's when I stopped watching through the window and started bringing clay and tools so I could work during her lessons. I sat in the outer waiting area with the other moms, talking and making rows of clay dolphin earrings or multi-colored cat pins at the same time.

The mother I remember most clearly was a native of Ireland, red haired, round-faced Regina. She told me stories of going to rowdy pubs as a young woman and how no one in her native country was homeless. "The government takes care of them all so they don't have to scrounge in garbage dumps and sleep on the street." I wondered what she thought of the homeless soup kitchen a mile away.

Regina had a daughter Lauren who was a very thin girl with some kind of chronic bowel disease, which was hereditary. She told me it could be life threatening and I thought, *how can this mother stand it?* I knew I would go to pieces if I had a child that ill. But apparently in between attacks that sent her to the hospital Lauren led a normal life and was strong enough to dance. Regina was philosophical about her daughter's condition, and looking back now I realized she'd already come to the place that I would eventually reach, where every day of your child's life is a gift.

After several months Cedar graduated to pointe shoes. We spent an hour in a ballet supply shop looking for the right fit. She picked out a pair then learned how to stuff it with wool batting so her poor toes could stand the pain of doing something they were never designed for.

Cedar's first few pointe lessons were agonizing, blister-producing affairs. She was shown how to tie the ribbons up her legs to lend more support but it didn't help.

In September Cedar tried out for the Sacramento Ballet's production of *The Nutcracker Suite.* We had an appointment at their studio, which was full of young girls from all the surrounding ballet schools standing in nervous little clumps waiting to be called.

Cedar and a row of similarly sized girls were put through basic ballet positions and movements and told that if they were chosen, they would find out in two weeks.

I think she heard by mail, because I don't remember an important phone call. "Congratulations! You have been chosen to play the part of one of the rats." Is that what was said? I'm sure not. But in some way that news was broken to Cedar who was not disappointed at all but couldn't wait for rehearsals, which started that very week at the Sacramento Community Center Theatre.

I have little memory of schlepping her to Sacramento for rehearsals. But during the hours of rehearsal, I sat in the car and made jewelry.

In December the performances began. Cedar's role was divided between herself and a company dancer, who lucky for Cedar was ambivalent about it so she picked up extra performances when he baled which happened with some frequency.

"The dressing rooms are beautiful!" Cedar was enthusiastic about the facilities, which of course, were designed for big name performers. But the work was hard and hot inside that cumbersome rat head with no peripheral vision.

My entire focus, like an enormous mental spotlight, had shifted to Cedar's professional debut.

I went to opening night with Andy, who swore he could tell which of the little rat minions was Cedar just by her body language and performance style. Even if he'd gotten it wrong, I loved him for saying that.

Ed and I watched the Nutcracker together the following weekend. I pointed Cedar out to him, but once they started their dance we lost her in the herd of identical costumes and masks.

28

CHRISTMAS

David arrived from L.A. just a few days before Christmas and to my chagrin just after *The Nutcracker Suite* had closed.

Our family took an afternoon trip to higher altitude looking for snow and found the perfect deserted spot to park on one side of an incline, just off the main road. David and Cedar chased each other down the hill with snowballs and loud whoops, and then built their first snowman since our trip to Flagstaff, Arizona eleven years earlier. That was in December too, visiting friends on our way back to California from Florida, and the first time our children had seen snow. Chris and Renee lived in the woods outside town, and their two little boys were the perfect introducers to winter. The four children romped in the snow, screaming and throwing snowballs at each other between skinny lodge pole pines. Ed and I sat by the fire drinking eggnog and eating home-made cookies with our friends. All four kids called us out to see their handiwork, a crooked little pile of three approximately round snow balls with a baby carrot nose and bits of frozen mud for the eyes and mouth. When we opened the door, Molly rushed out, then hopped lightly through several feet of the mysterious cold powder and meowed plaintively until I rescued her.

"Ed, do you realize this is the first time we've been in the snow since Flagstaff?"

"No, that can't be right," he said. But it was.

The bitterness and the dusk had seeped through our gloves and boots. Cedar said "Let's go! We're freezing!" and we piled back in the car. Our Volvo's relentless heating system melted the kids and they fell asleep on each other's shoulders driving home.

The next day Cedar, David and I went to Nevada City for some last minute Christmas shopping. I found David a Tintin T-shirt in a European import store and he bought a little booklet with blank handmade paper that he spent the whole night filling with his poetry to give to me on Christmas morning.

Every Christmas Eve I baked chocolate chip cookies for Santa, and left a note in my disguised handwriting for the kids. When they became teenagers this had continued, even the note.

Our Christmas tree was an ornamental record that started in 1986. The year before that we had all our possessions in storage in our laundry van, parked at a friend's house in California, while we were in Florida again. Someone from the city of Corte Madeira decided we were illegally parked and towed it. I suppose they had no way of contacting us because everything we owned was sold or given away.

But a few hand-made Christmas ornaments from early David and Cedar childhood had been stored somewhere else. Those hung on our tree now, alongside various clay angels, rejects from my jewelry making. Every branch had something on it, a bird in a basket from the swap meet in Marin County, a colorful kid design, a converted earring from the eighties.

When the kids were little, they both had a hand-crocheted stocking I had purchased from a team of grandmothers I'd met at a craft show. When they vanished, along with our laundry van, Cedar inherited the faded lace and jingle bell decorated stocking my mother had made for me as a child. It had a white "M" for *Merry* sewn on one side.

David ended up with a felt stocking that probably came from K-Mart, meant to be temporary but still in use.

Santa brought our children candy from the health food store. When the kids were young, they marveled at Santa Claus's perception. "How does he know we don't eat sugar?" David demanded.

"He's a magic guy," I answered reasonably.

Even when they figured out Santa was just an idea, they still piled on our bed every Christmas morning with their stockings, saying, "Guess what Santa brought us!" This year they waited till we were up, the only difference.

That Christmas day we drove to Sonoma County, where Rick and Terry had moved from San Francisco three years earlier. Peter had been married for two years and had a beautiful blond cherub of his own, now a year and a half old. He was named Sam after someone on his wife's side of the family.

Terry and I relished the idea of co-grandmothering this child, but she of course saw him a lot more than I did, which was only right. Back when Terry learned that Pete's wife was pregnant, she and Rick called us up and we had a four-way conference of amazement. Imagine us, grandparents!

Terry had decorated her townhouse with a big wreath and gold-colored garlands of little western men on horses. She had invited Pete's in-laws to Christmas dinner as well, so we had a big crowd in a small space full of delicious smells and wrapped boxes piled high on the coffee table.

I have a few photos of that event; Cedar, in her new short haircut, playing on the floor with a rosy-cheeked Sammy, Rick and Peter getting their instruments out to play, Pete's elderly in-laws looking bored, sitting on the good chairs.

The four of us spent the night at Terry and Rick's and the next morning went to the beach to take more photos. My favorite is one of Terry sitting cross-legged above me on a rock ledge. She is grinning and I think is looking off to the future we all assumed was ahead.

29

HALE-BOPP

In the Sierra Foothills, early spring was a winter continuation of rainy days. This turned the grass bright green in February, which always seemed wrong to me. I told Cedar, "I think we should call this season *sprinter*."

She made an elaborate groaning noise.

It was a muddy schlep to the garage, which had become a shelter for our winter stack of wood. I carried a sturdy cardboard box out to fill up with split logs and stepped gingerly around the puddles walking back.

Building a morning fire was my job, before Ed and Cedar woke up. I made fires the same way I cook. A little of that, (crumbled paper) a pinch of those (dry kindling) a helping of these (progressively larger wood pieces) placed in varying angles depending on shape and thickness. Like my recipes, it *usually* turned out well and the house would be toasty in thirty minutes.

On the west side of our property were five acres belonging to a man from New Jersey, whom we had never met. It was a jungle of blackberry bushes, poison oak and madrone trees, the bark shredding naturally in long red strips. It's where Cedar and I collected our kindling, carefully avoiding the poison oak, now leafless and benign looking. When Ed questioned my trespassing I told him, "We're clearing out our neighbor's underbrush, how can it be a bad thing?" The dead madrone wood was an excellent and practically instantaneous fire starter.

The only problem with a wood-heated house was the mess. We had a neat wooden box to keep the logs in, but it didn't hold enough for an entire day. So a dirty cardboard box with sagging sides and extra logs sat next to it. There were usually kindling bits scattered around on the rug, which had burnt spots right in front of the stove door where sparks had escaped.

I kept a pan of water on top—the air got pretty dry with that wood heat and California's naturally dry air. A little steam let into the room seemed to help. Once when the electricity went out, I even cooked a stew there.

We never did get a llama, but our neighbors across the road had a whole herd. When Cedar and I walked past their small ranch, we patted their arrogant muzzles, watching those ears carefully to gauge their mood. We were never spat upon.

But we had a lot of deer on our property. They became pests, eating up all the first flowers in early spring. I tried a couple of natural deterrents; panther piss I had purchased from our local organic nursery (to spray on the greenery) and soap bars I dangled from branches. Neither one had any effect whatsoever. The deer did leave the irises alone, some consolation.

One morning in late June, I found a deer in my vegetable garden. This was alarming. Had she leapt the fence? It was at least eight feet tall, supposedly deer-proof. Then I saw her entry, a shallow hole dug under the chicken wire. This persistent animal had pawed a place to burrow underneath the fence so she could reach my delectable young plants. Now she was trapped inside and panicking. I opened the gate and tried to chase her out, but she dashed crazily from side to side, trampling squash and tender new beans plants with her hooves. I screamed at her. I cried and begged her to leave and finally went inside the house, unable to watch the destruction of my garden for another second.

She eventually found her way out, after destroying weeks of new growth. I was soured on deer after that, and when Terry visited, oohing and aahing at their proximity to our house, she was surprised by how curmudgeonly I'd gotten about them.

When a friend found a freshly killed doe on the highway, she took the carcass to be processed for food and it didn't cause me a single sympathetic pang. But I still thought the spring fawns were cute and couldn't resist their baby calls that sounded surprisingly like "Ma!"

Gophers were another problem. A bean plant could disappear into the earth, being pulled straight down like a gag in a Bugs Bunny cartoon. I researched ways to eliminate them but they all seemed so cruel that I couldn't bring myself to do it. "I'll just plant more." I thought, but it was never enough.

Despite small annoyances, living in the country felt right to me. Walking outside on a spring day made me want to sing, and at night the sky was black and completely speckled with points of light; planets and stars that had been camouflaged by city lights for most of my life.

After midnight I sometimes heard an owl's hoo-hooing, and occasionally a night bird, calling in a lonesome minor key.

For many weeks during the spring of 1997, Cedar and I watched Hale-Bopp silently streaming through the eastern sky. We were on our way home from ballet class and the comet's motion, which appeared still to us, was just above the tree line on Rough and Ready Road. Ed phoned one night in April and said, "I see Hale-Bopp every night before I turn in." He was camping in a tent in Arizona, between art shows.

When I look back at my last mental snapshot of the comet, I imagine a *whooshing* sound as it escapes into space for another 2,380 years.

30

PHYLLIS

On spring and summer mornings I took my morning walk towards our neighbor's ranch. In half an hour I could reach their white fence and herd of pampered horses grazing in an emerald field.

Sometimes Cedar came with me and a beautiful bay mare would amble over so she could pat her nose. If I were alone on my walk, the horse pointedly ignored me.

We had neighbors separated by an acre or two all the way down the hill. Directly across from us, a friendly middle-aged couple raised emus, gigantic birds from Australia that skulked around in their large pen on sturdy legs. "Those hooded eyes remind me of terrorists," Cedar told me with a shiver. They were a little spooky looking, but their huge green eggs and striped babies were beautiful.

On our side of the road, to Cedar's delight, an eclectic bunch of quacking ducks daily waddled in a line heading down the hill in front of us. They were all different races; goofy looking ones with white topknots on their heads, mallards, even a black duck. They were all friends and muttered to each other as they veered off towards the neighbor's pond. Cedar still loved ducks, and dreamed of a duck pond of her own some day.

Another neighbor had a Shetland pony stallion that was in love with the Jenny who heehawed at him from across the road. It was scandalous; almost every spring his own dear wife gave birth to a winsome foal. He flirted shamelessly, neighing and running back and forth along his fence to attract her attention in the spring, the time of year he was especially randy.

One morning we disturbed a covey of quail. They were completely invisible until we startled them into a ruckus of feathers and upset. "It doesn't seem like much of a survival mechanism," Cedar commented.

On one of these walks, Cedar said, "I want to change my name."

"Oh. Do you know what you want to change it to?" I asked her cautiously. This wasn't the first time she'd brought this up

"I like the name Phyllis". Cedar didn't know about the madcap comedienne with the blond fright wig and a husband she called Fang.

"What other names have you thought about?"

"That's the one I really like," so I had to tell her about Phyllis Diller, the only Phyllis I knew of.

"She was a popular comedienne in the 1960s—very funny but pretty wacky looking. Crazy white hair and a loud voice, always making jokes about her husband. She called him Fang."

Cedar said, "I've never heard of her. The only Phyllis I know of was Phyllis Haver, an actress who did silent films with Mack Sennett in the 1920s. This Phyllis was adorable with short curly hair and a cute little bowed smile."

We walked on a while in silence, companionably. "What about the name Eva? That was my grandmother's name, you know."

"I know. It's a pretty name, but somehow it makes me think of the word 'evil.'"

I laughed. "Since my mother's sister's name was Eva Nell, Mom and her brothers teased her by calling her 'Evil Nell.'"

"That's funny," she looked up at me, smiling. "But I really do love the name Phyllis," she was staring at a cactus flower blooming beside the road—a waxy pink flower sitting incongruously atop a squat-spiked base right off the gravel shoulder.

"I think it would be impossible for me to get Phyllis Diller out of my mind."

"Oh well," she said, "At least 'Cedar' is a name directors will remember at casting calls." That was the last time she brought the subject up.

We'd reached the end of Rough and Ready Road, the place where the mare ambled over for a nose pat. "Hi, Sweetie," Cedar said. "I wish I had a carrot for you, or an apple." The horse neighed sweetly, rocking her huge head up and down in greeting.

31

EDUCATION

Cedar was bored despite dance lessons and daily hours spent writing and drawing. "I hate it here. I feel stuck."

We sat on the old swing set in our side yard and talked about how we could make things better. I rocked back and forth, pushing off on the hard dirt with my feet while Cedar stared despondently at the ground.

She wanted to act, and the local theatre group turned out to be a disappointingly clannish bunch. When we first moved to the area Cedar worked as an assistant to the actor playing Don Quixote in *Man of La Mancha*. She had a good time and became chums with them all, but she wasn't interested in theatre ambiance.

Finally she was cast in *Peer Gynt*, a minor production that closed after two performances.

We made extra trips to Sacramento when Cedar got a part in an adaptation of *Midsummer Night's Dream*. Rehearsals were in a school gym and the cast was not professional. But it was something.

Cedar played the part of Starveling the tailor who becomes "Moonshine" in the rough actors' very funny presentation to royalty in the last act. Cedar treated her small role seriously and worked her seven lines up to a believable cockney character.

After the play closed, the director sent her a card with this note:

"You 'disfigure' the person of Moonshine as well as it's ever been done. Hope to see you on many more stages."

She fell in love with Shakespeare's poetry and perception of life. I remember her writing a short story around that time based on a young girl who disguises herself as a boy so she can perform in the Globe theatre, circa 1590. She never finished the story, but I still have its beginning somewhere in the stack of yellow-lined writing tablets tucked away in her closet.

A little while after that talk on the swings, Cedar had a brief encounter with public high school, a short-lived minor disaster. In the mornings she walked through the dusk to a bus stop at the next crossroad, then traveled the two miles to school and sat through classes designed for other people's children.

"Our history class spent the whole period watching the O. J. Simpson murder trial," she complained to me one day. That wasn't the worst of it though. "Kids cheat so casually, like that's all they know how to do. They don't care a whit about learning. And in between classes they talk about taking drugs and drinking on the weekends."

In October, just six weeks later, I had a meeting with the principal and told her I was taking Cedar out of the high school. She warned me against it, insisting that Cedar just needed time to adjust to life as a freshman.

Adjust to what? I wondered. I thanked her for her concern and signed the papers to my daughter's freedom.

We talked to the local home schooling supervisor, a mild-mannered gentleman with a ginger mustache who made it clear I was on my own to devise a curriculum.

Cedar and I spent a lot of time at the library researching ancient cultures, Egyptian was still her favorite, but I felt like a faker. I was no teacher and I certainly didn't know what I was doing when it came to higher mathematics.

A friend of ours told us about The California Ranch School run by educators John and Carlynn McCormick. The school was in Perris, just south of Los Angeles.

They were using the study methods of L. Ron Hubbard, something Cedar was familiar with. Joy of joys, they had a real curriculum for home school students, with check-sheets for each subject. Every line on each check-sheet had a different study assignment, drill or essay to be completed before being signed off by the student. This way Cedar could study at her own pace.

It included all the basics required by California law for high school, but The California Ranch School actually required the student have a hundred percent understanding before graduating. There was no squeaking by with a "C average".

Cedar wrote her observations on the public school system in this paper for one of her assignments after she had just turned fifteen:

Public School Tragedy

"Let us say, if you will, that our public school system is a figurative battlefield (and not all too figurative at that!) and your little Joey is the soldier. Only little Joey, having been brought up in this sort of life, doesn't know any better, and so he marches back and forth with his artillery, like a time bomb waiting to explode.

"One of these days he sees all the other soldiers charge, and so he charges as well, only to be felled along with the majority of his comrades. It is not such an esoteric analogy. Perhaps even, the child would grasp it better than the adult. How can this be? Because with all fairness and due respect to the parent, our educational system has been

sliding so rapidly in the past few decades, that even when you attended school, imperfect as it was, it stood worlds above today's institutions.

"Think back to when you were in grade school; did a teacher ever once have to discuss the dangers of drugs and sexually transmitted diseases? Unheard of, right? Did your high school distribute condoms in an ineffective attempt to stop teenage pregnancies? Not on your life! But this, this is the key, and I want you to read these words carefully: did a man spouting ludicrous psychobabble ever tell your parents that because you cried after losing a baseball game, or liked to run outdoors, or couldn't quite grasp multiplication yet, that you had some cockeyed 'mental deficiency,' slap some psych label on you and pump you full of drugs to the point where you were 'quiet?' If you think I exaggerate, go and visit the office of your school therapist and see for yourself the tomes written about fraudulent mental diseases, and the poison they call drugs, which 'cure' them.

"However, the real purpose of this article is not to impeach school psychologists but to speak as the voice of a child to the parents of today. I have gone to these public schools before, not for long, admittedly, but long, enough to experience what I sincerely hope your child never does.

"What seems to be absent above all else is simple common sense. It doesn't take a genius to figure if you don't understand a word to look it up in the dictionary, and it

certainly doesn't take an Einstein to figure that if one is in an English or History class, that is what one studies.

"For those parents who know how degraded it's gotten, but are wary of pulling their children out for fear that if they don't receive a 'proper' education they shall surely perish, let me make a point which I hope will help you to see the light. Probably the majority of geniuses and impressive historical figures did not receive a formal education. This does not mean they went uneducated. It means simply that they sought knowledge in different and more effective ways.

"If I can be any sort of example, my education has been extremely chopped and spliced together. A year at this school, three years at that, a year of not doing much of anything; and I still match my knowledge to any fifteen year old or high school graduate who grew rancid as she fermented away in the public schools for twelve years. I do not propose that every child travel to Timbuktu before they reach the age of ten, or that every 6th grader be a budding Aristotle, but I'm quite convinced a study of students outside the public school system would reveal a distinctly higher level of learning.

"Now for those parents still unconvinced, I should like to relate to you a few stories from my experience in a small town 'top' public high school. Keep in mind that this is merely skimming the very surface of the cesspool; I made it a point of not allowing myself to act the little sheep or soldier, as it were, who followed along with the rest. But

take my word for it, there are more flocks in these schools than one would care to imagine.

"I will begin with my English class and you will no doubt see how atrocities such as 'Ebonics' could ever have been invented. Basic fundamentals have long since departed and been replaced with a psychology based education, which produces a society dumber than dirt.

"Indeed, I felt the majority of the time that I knew more than my teacher who had a degree in literature. We received all sorts of enlightening assignments to play with, such as different techniques to guessing the meanings of words (apparently the dictionaries were for pressing dry rose petals or some such thing) and we viewed such educational films as the O. J. Simpson murder trial, or a horrible motion picture called "Camp Nowhere," which could at least have lived up to its name, stayed that way, and been nowhere to be found. All of this, of course, was entirely irrelevant to our studies, which proceeded at a pace a snail could easily have rivaled.

"Looking at my fellow students, especially in Algebra, one got the impression that the poor things were lost somewhere back in the 1st grade and wouldn't have known an integer if it walked up and bit them on the hinder. I can forgive the students for their basic illiteracy. That is simply the uniform result of the schools these days, but because they are so stupefied and numb from years of poor education, they turn their attention to a game; any game will do. This is where the druggie punks, gangs, and such *enter into it, and it is dangerously catching. The natural sheep phenomenon of young people trying to fit in has a devastating effect on otherwise ethical boys and girls.*

"When one is fully informed of the state of the schools, it seems there would be few who would continue to subject their children to it. As a fifteen year old to the parents of children in public schools, or considering the enrollment of their children in these battlefields masquerading as educational institutions, I strongly urge you to reconsider."

In less than a year Cedar would complete an entire four-year high school program.

"I'd like to go to Perris and meet my teachers before I graduate," Cedar told us toward the end of her study program. Carlyn was happy to have her come, so we packed her bags and drove her there in person. She finished all her studies in two weeks and graduated as valedictorian of her class.

This is an excerpt from that address:

"We are the new generation. The future lies very much in our own hands, in the hands of the young and the brave, and those courageous enough to live their dreams in reality.

"If all my generation could have as comprehensive an education as my fellow California Ranch School graduates, the future would look very bright indeed. And perhaps it does at that."

MOLLY'S GOODBYE

When we moved to Rough and Ready in 1994, Molly was twelve years old.

At first she was suspicious of all that space. It took David and Cedar on their hands and knees, a can of tuna and lots of encouraging noises from both of them, to entice her to slip through the kitty door onto the redwood deck outside. It was her gateway to a new world, and her first entrance was a low skulk, yellow eyes wide with alarm.

Before long Molly's vision expanded. There were no loose dogs to terrorize her, she had an entire gravel driveway to roll around on and there were fascinating turkey families gobbling their way across our property on a regular basis.

These she watched from the safety of the deck, fluffed up and vibrating with predatory, but stationary excitement.

In the spring, Molly liked to nap on the granite boulder underneath the lilac trees in our front yard. "She smells like lilacs!" Cedar announced after kissing her head.

Cedar and Molly were best friends, but Cedar left any accidents, fur balls and vomit for me to clean up. Thus their affection for each other was untainted by worldly things.

Whenever Cedar sat down and Molly was anywhere near, a crescendo-ing "brrrrt!" would accompany her gentle lap leap. "Molly!" Cedar would say in mock surprise.

Molly loved to eat. She was supposed to be fed daily at five, but she started asking for dinner around three o' clock, making encouraging sounds and looking over her shoulder while heading for the kitchen. "Mol-lee!" Cedar scolded her gently, "You have to wait!" After a while, her dinner hour was compromised to four.

But when Molly turned fifteen the liver ailment she had suffered from as a young cat reappeared. She declined so rapidly that Cedar had to help her onto her bed at night, her appetite astonishingly vanished and she had bathroom accidents at random. The veterinarian gently suggested euthanasia due to her age.

"Oh Mommy, I'm so worried about her."

"We'll just keep her comfortable and love her and see if she can get through this," I said.

Since Molly didn't appear to be in great pain, we kept her home. Veterinary visits terrified her and it didn't feel right that she should end her days under fluorescent lights in an unfamiliar room.

When her last night arrived and she was too ill to move, I slept on the living room couch beside her blanket-lined box. Cedar wanted to be with her but I insisted she get a good night's sleep. I stayed awake, petting Molly's heaving side as she struggled between this happy lifetime and whatever came next.

When she died in the wee hours, I gently closed her eyes and covered her with a soft baby blanket.

Cedar was up early. "How's Molly doing?" she asked sadly.

"She died last night," I answered and Cedar hugged me, crying.

"Oh Mommy, I miss her!" I rubbed her back and held her for a long time, until she asked to see the body.

We pulled back the blanket and Cedar gave her a last pet. "She's so soft."

Cedar wanted to bury her Egyptian style, with everything she'd need for her next life. We found a sturdy box, wrapped Molly in the baby blanket and put her gently inside.

Cedar put her favorite toy and a can of tuna beside her, along with a note telling Molly how much she loved and missed her. We sealed the box and buried it in the back, just behind the irises and where the grass grew long and green every spring.

33

EAST AGAIN

Ed was in Florida again, working on some advanced training in our church. He told me he might be gone for up to six months, but I accepted this with equanimity. Magic Zoo called for a lot of traveling by Ed in those days of art shows and customer appointments in San Jose and I was used to his absence.

When we were juried into two Florida art shows at the same time in February of 1998, I flew out to do one of them. Molly had just died and Cedar would be staying with friends while I was gone.

Ed was living in a tiny studio apartment over a garage in a section of Clearwater called Harbor Oaks. The neighborhood was pleasant. Giant oak trees festooned with grey green Spanish moss were planted majestically in front of two-story houses like comfortable old friends. I remembered this area from when the kids were little and we took walks to the pier watching for skinny gar and jellyfish in the murky water below.

Now we were alone, three thousand miles from both our children. We held hands, walking past a large brick house with a cascade of hot-pink bougainvillea pouring over the fence. I felt dizzy, like the earth was tipping sideways and I was sliding the wrong way. "I wish the kids were with us."

Ed squeezed me and kissed the back of my neck. "I know," he said.

The next morning we set off way before dawn so Ed could drop me at my art show and drive sixty miles further down the road to set up his. It was still dark when I wandered onto the fair grounds pulling the giant gun case that held my tent and the luggage full of jewelry behind me.

I had no idea where to go, but already there were cheery volunteers with flashlights directing artists to their booth spaces. I smelled hot coffee, which I knew I shouldn't drink but always drowned my sorrows in when I did a show alone. I poured myself a steaming cup and added a generous helping of cream.

As soon as the sky lightened I fastened poles and vinyl together till the final hoist up, when I needed help getting my tent in the air. My neighbors were wonderful people, as they almost always seem to be at outdoor art shows. "Sure, no problem! My name's Al. What do you make?" As we raised the poles this burly middle-aged stranger chatted nonstop.

The dew was starting to evaporate and white booths were springing up like oversized mushrooms in neat rows.

The show promoters seemed to have done their job because customers were wandering down the rows by nine, middle-aged tourists with tropical shirts, white shorts and little battery operated personal fans, or young parents with tattoos and toddlers. One woman pushed a Yorkshire terrier in a stroller right into my booth.

That evening Ed picked me up and we headed for our motel which was midway between the two shows. We looked for somewhere to eat on the way there and found a local fish place. I talked while we sipped lemony iced tap water and waited for our food.

"I really miss you. You might be here another half a year and Cedar is going crazy in Rough and Ready. Maybe we should find someone we could rent our house to and move here for a while." It was one of those half-baked thoughts I immediately regretting saying out loud, because Ed pounced right on it.

"That's a great idea!" he exclaimed. "You and Cedar can drive out here together and…"

"Drive all the way from California, just the two of us?" I couldn't believe he meant that.

"You know I can't leave now and you're completely capable of driving out yourself. It would be fun."

I sulked, but Ed was unrelenting. "Look, you can have someone help you pack the truck and…."

"What truck?"

"You might as well bring our furniture if we'll be renting someplace in Clearwater. There's no use in getting all new stuff. At least bring the beds and the bookcases." This was unbelievable. What had I been thinking, bringing this up?

I mulled this over at the show the next day. It was true Cedar needed a change. She had graduated from her high school program, her last play had wrapped and now Molly was gone. I thought she still enjoyed ballet, but the last time we'd driven there she told me, "I started ballet too late to make it as a professional dancer. I'm getting tired of this drive and the lessons are going nowhere for me."

I called her that night. "Daddy and I were thinking about moving the two of us to Clearwater, so we could all be together."

"That sounds great! How soon can we leave?" Her instant enthusiasm for this barely formed plan disarmed me.

"Are you sure that's what you'd want to do?"

"Mom, I want to get out of here. There has to be more going on in the Tampa area. And I miss Dad."

When I got home the next week her excitement was undiminished. "How soon are we leaving?" she asked as soon as we hugged hello.

Back when Cedar attended charter school in the eighth grade, I'd met Margo, a tall, handsome woman with a teenage son named Joshua. Margo had been an international model in the 1980s, and then had a baby boy with a married man in New York. "That sort of thing went on all the time," she told me. "But I was young and was convinced he loved me." Of course she was on her own with the child, and ended up living first in Oakland, then just a few miles away from us, in Grass Valley. Margo and I carpooled our kids to school and became friends. When I bumped into her at the co-op I told her we were moving to Florida for a while.

"What about your house?"

"I want to find someone to take care of it for a few years," I told her.

"I'd love to live there, if I could afford it. I've just started a daycare business and it would be perfect for me."

We talked it over and settled on a below market rent; I wanted to make sure she could pay it. "She's really caretaking it for us," I reasoned with Ed.

I wasn't much of a landlady. Her rent didn't pay for half the mortgage payments. But I told her the daycare business had to be conducted somewhere else. "I have this image of a three-year-old tripping in the gravel and banging his head on a boulder," I told her. "I can't be worried about other people's children from three thousand miles away." She understood.

Two weeks later I rented a Ryder van, which seemed more manageable to me than a truck. But I was bothered by the lack of windows in the back, and during the entire trip I felt blindfolded when I had to back up.

Cedar and I packed the van by ourselves. It took a day, but for a week before that we had boxed up all we were taking and moved everything else into one of the little rooms attached to the garage.

Moving the furniture wasn't easy, but when one of us suddenly dropped the corner of a bookcase or crashed into a doorway walking backwards we both laughed. This was an activity made to order for The Little Nerd and her mom; we stayed in character for hours at a time.

The bigger pieces were left behind, sold to Margo for a song. We still brought enough stuff to completely fill that van without any wiggle room at all. Ed's always been the master packer of our family but his putting together the 3-D puzzles of our possessions during years of moving around must have rubbed off, and we did a pretty decent job.

34

THE TRIP

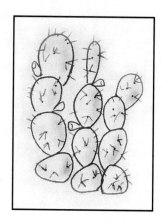

We had planned to visit David in Los Angeles during our California exit, but he was working on a project that could not be interrupted. This news was upsetting, but it did mean I wouldn't have to navigate that beast of a vehicle down Interstate 5 and into the heart of L.A.

We took another route, all the way down 99 to Bakersfield and then weaving east to 15 south. When we hit I-10 we stayed on it across the entire country. Cedar and I drove for ten hours a day through the Arizona desert past saguaro cacti marching up dry hills like headless green stick men, chubby arms roundly reaching for the clear blue sky.

Every couple of days I called Terry to tell her where we were. "We just rented a motel room in a dusty little town in

Arizona. It's the first time Cedar's seen tumbleweed, and the only place to eat dinner is a Dairy Queen!"

Terry laughed. "I wish I were with you!" Ed didn't have a cell phone or a land line, either. He had to call Terry from a pay phone to find out how our trip was going.

We switched the radio from classical music to classic rock and back again. Before this trip Cedar never listened to 'fifties and 'sixties music, but it was the closest thing to her beloved deco decades and it did pretty well. I loved it, singing along with the Beatles and Chuck Berry as loudly as I could. "Stretching my voice muscles," I told Cedar who encouraged me.

We never looked in those motel coupon books for where to stay at night, the way Ed and I do when we travel—that was much too organized for us. Cedar and I drove until we were pooped, then looked for someplace with a decent rate advertised on the freeway and hopefully a place to eat that we could walk to from there. At a Texas roadhouse we had grilled vegetables cut into little sticks, with a juicy piece of grilled chicken taking up most of the plate. We slept in clean, soft beds in the family-owned motel next door.

Cedar and I pretended to be macho truck drivers. "Wildcat, this is Big Bob. Speed bump ahead. Over."

"Roger that, Big Bob."

One time we parked in the trucker's section of a rest stop for the sole purpose of laughing at our dinky van sandwiched between two gigantic rigs.

Texas took two days to drive through. The second day I was irritable navigating the twisty turns of I-10 through Houston. *Why didn't Ed warn me?* I thought nonsensically. I swore out loud as I almost missed our exit for the second time.

After that it was pretty easy, sailing through Louisiana, where we took a break from classic rock on the radio and listened to Cajun music in American-accented French. We planned to stop in New Orleans, and I bravely pulled off the freeway near the French Quarter and glided right into the perfect parking space at a corner, right on Bourbon Street. It was early afternoon and still pretty tame, no rowdy college kids or scantily clad women dancing in the windows, yet.

We ate lunch on the balcony of a Cajun restaurant, the wooden floor slanting precariously toward the street below, a flimsy wrought-iron fence all that separated us from the festive New Orleans air. Afterwards we walked in and out of shops, thumbing through posters of old jazz greats. Cedar bought a photograph of Josephine Baker wearing practically nothing—just a few sparkles and that famous seductive grin. It was from her French cabaret days in the '20s and '30s, where she achieved fame and fortune dancing in banana skirts for French gentlemen.

When we got back on the Freeway we drove straight to Pensacola Florida.

"What did you think of New Orleans?" I asked Cedar.

"I loved it!"

I was wiped out by the time we stopped at a Comfort Inn in around ten p.m. "What's the rate for two adults?" I asked the bleary-eyed clerk. But it was too high. I walked away, rolling my eyes at Cedar.

"Wait. I think I can help you." I must have looked awfully bedraggled because he ended up giving me the room for a Motel 6 price. Maybe he was afraid I'd fall asleep driving to a real Motel 6, burdening his conscience forever.

We slept well that night. Clearwater was in our sights, a few inches to the right on the map from where we were, then straight south.

35

TERRY

We turned south off 10, heading toward Tampa on I-75. For the first time I noticed all the antique shop signs on the Freeway, but by then there was no time to stop. Clearwater was still at least three hours away.

I'd made a careful map of how to get through Tampa, read to me by Cedar as we navigated the changes. When we sailed across the causeway to Clearwater I could feel butterflies all the way from my stomach to my heart.

"We're almost there!" I shouted happily.

We found a place to park in downtown Clearwater, across from the building where Ed was studying. "It feels weird to be back here," Cedar told me. The last time she had been in Clearwater, she was only six. "I remember the air being wet, and tons of green plants everywhere you looked. It feels just the same."

Ed walked out of his classroom and spotted Cedar leaning against the Ryder truck. "Dad!"

"Baby Girl!" She wrapped her arms around him and after a mutual bear hug, Ed lifted her off the ground with a grunt. They'd been apart for close to five months.

I gave Ed a kiss and bragged about our trip. "We made it! It took less than a week. Isn't that incredible? And not a single scratch on the truck." I patted it fondly.

We were hungry, but the eating choices within walking distance were pretty limited. There was a Cajun cafeteria where a Korean couple scooped up fatty chicken bits cooked in Louisiana spices, spoonfuls of red beans punctuated with sausage and overcooked cabbage.

The other possibility was a 24-hour breakfast place that was so smoky the glass windows were permanently stained with nicotine residue. We went for the Cajun, picking sausage bits from our red beans and rice.

"Merry, our rental house isn't ready yet, so we have to stay in an apartment for a little while."

"What? I thought everything was set. We have to unload the van and take it back to Ryder!" I protested.

Ed explained he had arranged to unload everything into the side porch of our future house. It would be safe, he assured me. I sighed. Oh well, at least he'd found us a home and eventually we'd move in. I was too tired to worry about it anyway.

The apartment where we would stay in the meantime belonged to a friend of Ed's who had gone out of town for a few weeks. We had a bedroom and Cedar would sleep on a day bed in the main room.

The three of us took a walk along Edgewater Drive that first evening, just two blocks from the apartment. Gangly palm trees were silhouetted against the pink sunset now spread to the eastern sky, and Clearwater Bay had turned a deep sapphire blue. The temperature had dropped a few degrees and was almost comfortable.

When we got back the phone was ringing. It was Terry checking in. Rick was on the phone too, which surprised me. Usually our "conference calls" were for really important things. She asked "How was the last part of your trip?"

I told them about our afternoon in New Orleans and described our sunset walk. "The shoreline here is beautiful—it looks exactly like those old postcards, only without the pastel colorizing."

"Merry, I don't want you to worry, but when I had my last checkup the doctor found out the cancer was back, and it's in my bones."

"What? Oh, Terry…" my voice trailed off.

"It isn't an instant death sentence. He told me with treatment I could live for years, long enough to rock several more grandchildren to sleep." Terry once told me the worst part about having cancer was making everyone she loved feel bad.

Even Rick had nothing funny to lighten the moment with. We quietly wound down the conversation to a "We'll call you as soon as we've moved into our house and have a phone."

"What's wrong?" Ed watched my expression as I hung up. "It's Terry—the cancer's back." I started to cry and then Cedar was crying, and Ed had both of us to comfort.

"Tell me what she said exactly."

I ignored him, suddenly furious with Terry. "Why didn't she visit her oncologist last winter? In January she told me the area of the mastectomy had been bothering her. She decided that it was nothing but a pulled muscle from aerobics class."

Ed let me fume, watching me quietly. I looked at Cedar who had stopped crying. "What did she say?" Ed asked me again. I had calmed down, trying to remember her words.

"She said the doctor thought she could live for quite a while and that it wasn't time to give up. That she had time to rock more grandkids to sleep." I looked at Ed. "But you know how she's always trying to make everyone else feel better."

He gave me a hopeful smile. "There's nothing wrong with that. And maybe she's right."

36

FLORIDA

After two weeks we moved into our house, a 1920s era two bedroom that sat on the corner of Drew Street at a major intersection near downtown. The house was charming, original yellow-tiled bathroom with a claw foot tub, tiny bedrooms with built-in bookcases and a screened-in porch off the living room.

It would have been fine somewhere else, off that street. In Rough and Ready I woke up to the incongruously sweet sounds of birds ferociously defending their territories, but here their songs would have been drowned by traffic noise and loud rap music blaring a few yards from our bedroom window.

Less than a week after we moved in I had to go to Michigan; The Magic Zoo was in an art show just outside the museum in Flint, and I was flying there by myself for three days. I didn't want to leave Cedar so soon after moving. "I'll be fine, Mom. I'll get a lot of drawing and writing done while you're gone."

An article in the local paper caught Cedar's interest. It was about a woman named Mandy Wildman who taught acting lessons in downtown Clearwater. She was a British actress recently moved here from L.A. but before that had been in a popular TV series in South Africa. Best, she'd been trained in the theatre in London. She taught lessons once a week in a Clearwater facility. "I can't wait to check it out!" Cedar grinned at me.

My flight was early the next morning. I waited outside before dawn for the airport van. Five a.m. and it must have been ninety degrees already.

I hated flying to shows by myself. The whole time I was in the air I was nervous. Flying made me a little jittery, but the real problem started after the plane landed.

At baggage claim, I scanned the crowd for a burly-looking man I could entreat to lift my seventy-pound gun case full of poles and fold-up tables off the conveyor belt. The one time I attempted it myself, I'd fallen backwards on my butt, laughing to mask my pain and embarrassment.

But I was lucky in Michigan. The airport was teeming with bored porters, and I grabbed one before the first pass of the suitcases. This kindly young man not only grabbed my gear off the luggage belt, but pushed it to the car rental line, waited while I filled out the papers, rolled his dolly to where the rental car shuttle picked me up, then loaded it on the van.

Maybe it was for a good tip (which of course I gave him) but he earned every penny and brightened my day besides. I felt hopeful and by the time I got my car loaded and headed out the gate towards Flint, I was pretty calm.

I set up my booth that Friday afternoon. It was as hot as Florida had been the day I left. "Hi, my name's Merry," I introduced myself to the young couple with the booth next door. He was still hanging canvases while his wife nursed their newborn in the back corner of their booth.

A few minutes later, before I could ask for help hoisting my booth in the air he shouted, "Well, we're taking off. See you tomorrow!" His wife smiled at me and he zipped up their tent and picked up the diaper bag—narrowly missing the ferocious mosquito hordes that I had to battle for another hour.

The show promoters here took care of their artists. They distributed water bottles on Saturday afternoon and even threw a party for us that night. Monetary awards were given to prize-winning artists along with large, gaudy ribbons to display in their booths on Sunday. I didn't win a prize for my jewelry and wondered vaguely what the judge was thinking when she made her pass through my booth earlier, absently sticker-ing my sign with a little green circle to prove she'd been there.

I had a good show, ribbon or no.

I flew home the day after it ended, going perfectly backwards, ending up on the sidewalk outside our house at five in the afternoon, dropped off by the same driver who had picked me up.

Cedar was on the phone when I walked in the door. This was a little surprising because who did she know in Clearwater? She was speaking in a British accent and calling the person on the other end of the line "Henry." She looked at me and smiled, said goodbye to her new friend then said "Hi Baby!" giving me a hug.

Ed and I both called Cedar "Baby Girl" from the time she was born, and when she got old enough to be consciously funny she called me the same thing, with variations. We had many names for each other; Puddy Cat, (that one started with Molly), Pumpkin Fish, Fishcake, Doodlebug.

"Who were you *talking* to?" I emphasized the "talking" because she knew that I knew this was a surprising development in just three days.

"His name is Gily. I met him at the acting class and we really hit it off!" She made it clear this was a friendship thing, not a romance in the making, and that Henry was a character they'd made up.

"So tell me about the class!" I patted the couch inviting her to sit down next to me.

"I love Mandy! She's not a stuck up 'know-it-all'. She was totally encouraging and wants me to join an improv group she's forming with some of the other students."

"When can I meet her?" I asked.

"You can pick me up after my next class on Tuesday and I'll introduce you."

The building where Mandy taught acting was under construction. Dry wall separated it into sections and the floor was plain concrete. Her students were gathered in the largest room. Cedar introduced me to Gily—short, good-looking and Israeli. He had a wide grin and shook my hand heartily.

"And, this is Laura!" A tall, Rubenesque woman with thick black curls framing her face smiled at me.

"Are you an actress, too?"

I laughed. "Oh no, I'm just part of Cedar's fan club."

Cedar caught Mandy's eye as she swished towards us in a floor length flowered skirt.

"You must be Cedar's mom! You have a very talented daughter." Her blue eyes were intense, honest. Mandy was attractive; she wore her blonde hair long and spoke with a shadow of an English accent.

"What did you think of everyone?" Cedar was watching me while we drove the few blocks towards home.

"I think they're great. I can't believe you met up with this group so quickly. Good job!"

"I know—I'm so happy" Cedar squeezed my hand and sunk into the upholstery with a satisfied sigh.

THE APARTMENT

Our landlord, who lived next door, seemed to have a "thing" for Cedar. She wrote this in her diary:

"My parents travel a lot for their art shows, and this strange specimen lived in a little building next to the house, so my dad casually mentioned that it would be nice if he made sure I was all right while they were away. His name was René, a French Canadian. Well, he got the idea that sixteen was old enough and took me to the beach, and was saying things about it being romantic, and referring to people our age, as if our ages were anywhere close."

Cedar was 5 feet 7 inches tall, dark and slim with a heart-shaped face and expressive brown eyes. She wore her hair in a 1920s-style bob, like silent film star Louise

Brooks—which really made her stand out in a crowd. Once when Cedar and I walked down a Clearwater street and a car load of young men wolf-whistled and made lewd comments in her direction, I shouted back "I'm her *mother*! Leave her alone!" It was gratifying seeing their shocked faces just before they turned a corner.

It took me a while to calm down but Cedar was laughing. "Mom, that was great!"

Living downtown was convenient and seemed relatively safe, but I hadn't slept well from the first night. Ed could snore through anything, including, to my earlier chagrin, newborns crying in the middle of the night. But he was sympathetic. "Okay, we'll look for something on a quieter street." The other reason to move was our love-struck landlord. After Cedar's last report I wasn't comfortable leaving her alone.

"Hey look at this," Ed was reading the local classifieds. "There's a two bedroom apartment in a great area of town for six-fifty a month including utilities. We wouldn't have to stay there forever, but it would give us time to either finish up in Clearwater and go back to Rough and Ready, or buy a home here."

"I guess it can't hurt to look at it." I was unenthusiastic about this potential return to apartment dwelling.

The three of us drove to the east side of town, near busy Highway 19. It was a big complex—brick red buildings with a swimming pool in the middle. There was a community meeting area with fresh coffee for the tenants and a shelf full of paper back books you could borrow anytime. This is where Jane and Jerry had their office. They were the apartment managers, a rotund couple with lilting Minnesotan accents.

"Yes, there's an apartment available just across from the pond. It's upstairs so it'll be quiet. The couple living below is retired. Would you like to see it?" Jane was reaching for the key.

Her husband plodded upstairs while we followed, explaining that the place would be getting new carpets before it was rented. It was spotless. Freshly painted, a stacked washer and dryer in the kitchen behind a louver door, two bedrooms, each with a bath. The living room was small, but it had windows abutting a gnarled grey oak. Two squirrels chased each other in a diagonal blur up the trunk.

Twenty yards away white egrets and grey herons waded in the pond, eyes bright and bills pointed like daggers towards unaware fish prey. "Is that an otter?" I shouted. Just beyond the birds a sinuous shape curved out of the water and disappeared.

"Yeah, we do get them from time to time," Jerry chuckled, then said, "Well, I'll let you folks decide. Come on back to the office when you make up your minds."

Ed looked at us. "Well?"

"I like it!" said Cedar.

"It's a little far from downtown," I pointed out to her. "What do you think, Ed?" I was still watching the pond.

Ed wasn't sure. He'd have to do a lot of driving back and forth to class, maybe twice a day. On the other hand, the apartment was clean and inexpensive. When Ed and I were traveling to shows, Cedar would have neighbors nearby at night, and Jerry and Jane lived in a house right next door to the property.

"Let's take it."

We filled out an application and paid a small fee to reserve it. When we moved in a week later, the new carpet had been laid—dark teal, the color Cedar and I had chosen.

Cedar covered the walls in her room with framed movie magazine drawings from the 1920s, a black and white poster of Laurel and Hardy in prison stripes, and a deco calendar we'd found at Border's. She was tired of her pastel bed quilt and saved her money for a solid black bedspread.

Because it was such a small apartment, I stuffed possessions never to be unpacked in a little place behind our couch and above Cedar's room in an attic-like space not really designed for storage. Ed stood on a stool and pushed boxes I handed him into the void above his head.

My studio was a drafting table set up in the corner by the big oak tree, facing the television so I could watch videos while I worked. A long, low dresser behind me, against the wall, held all my clay and supplies.

We replaced our king-sized bed with a queen and that was a good thing because our bedroom had the Magic Zoo Office in it as well. This consisted of a metal filing cabinet, a desk, and at least five boxes full of books, lined up in a row outside our bathroom and against the wall. That's how I broke my little toe one morning, rushing from the shower to answer the phone.

It was a quiet apartment, at least the side Ed and I were on. But Cedar could hear the young man who shared a wall with her bedroom, especially on Friday nights when he partied with his girlfriend. It wasn't too much of a problem for her since she often stayed up till three in the morning writing, and by that time even they had fallen asleep.

38

FRIENDS

Laura and Cedar were close friends now. Cedar spent Friday nights at her house watching movies and in between they had long phone conversations or went on impromptu shopping excursions. Laura was almost two decades older than Cedar, and married to a sweet, soft-spoken man named Dan. Back then they had no children.

Once I knew her a little better, Laura confessed she was worried I'd be jealous of their friendship. But I had no insecurities about my daughter's affection, and I was perfectly content to share it with Laura. Not content, relieved. Cedar could be pretty intense; passionate about the decay of education, concerned with how art was used to propagandize in modern day film, upset about the general ethics level of young people her age. Large, kind Laura, with her big smile and easygoing humor was the perfect antidote.

Slim, soft-spoken Wayne was Laura's pal before Cedar appeared in Clearwater; now the three of them were inseparable. They were budding screenplay writers, and when Laura developed a script based on her chess expertise, Wayne and Cedar helped her polish some of the dialogue. The result was Laura's first screenplay, titled *In the Open*.

The script would be the first film produced by Wild Heart Studios, the company formed by Mandy Wildman and Laura Sherman. Cedar was playing the part of Ricki, a die-hard tomboy. Halfway through the film she becomes enamored of a dashing young chess player and willingly undergoes a miracle transformation into a charming and sophisticated young lady.

Cedar was doing her own writing. She started work on a film script at night after eight hours of rehearsals and filming for *In the Open*. After dinner, she shut her bedroom door and worked until the wee hours, scribbling away furiously by hand on yellow-lined pads of paper. The next morning we'd tiptoe around till she emerged around noon, yawning and asking, "What's for breakfast?"

"How did filming go yesterday?"

"I'm learning a lot about acting for film. Everything is so much subtler than the stage, like not making big motions or expressions. The film picks it all up and it looks exaggerated if you don't do it right."

We talked about how timing works, what makes something funny, what overacting is. We watched so many films together that our personal observations merged. What makes Laurel and Hardy's slapstick funny and not the cruder humor of The Three Stooges? (At least from our viewpoint). Laurel and Hardy played their roles straight. They became those two characters in earnest, while Curly, Mo and Larry were too intentionally funny. Things like that.

During filming of *In the Open,* Ed and I had separate art shows to attend. We were gone for several days. I returned before Ed and found Cedar acting uncharacteristically nervous.

"Are you upset about something?"

"Mom, I have to talk to you."

We sat down together on the only piece of comfortable furniture in the living room, the tiny flower print loveseat facing the windows.

"I've gotten involved with someone."

"What do you mean involved?" I was alarmed.

"We had sex."

She hugged me and apologized as I wept like a woman betrayed which is how I felt at that moment. "Did you use protection?" I managed to surface long enough to be practical.

"No. He didn't use a condom."

"What? Cedar, what in the world were you thinking?" Cedar was still a child, this proved it to me. And I had been a negligent mother, not practical enough to warn my daughter about the dangers of plain old sex in the '90s, not to mention unprotected sex. I'd thought of her as an adult, making rational decisions in all areas, which I painfully realized now wasn't true.

"Who is this guy?" She told me his name. He was an actor in the movie, someone I'd never met. He was twenty years old, three years older than Cedar and she was not his first girl. I thought about AIDS and pregnancy and told her that he had to get an AIDS test right away.

"Oh mom, that's so embarrassing. How can I ask him to do that?" I assured her that if she didn't ask him, then I would.

Ed and I spoke that night, whispering together before we went to sleep. "I need to speak to her too, from a male perspective." As parents, we were trying to salvage a little dignity between us.

I said "I feel like such an idiot."

Ed hugged me, saying nonsensically, "It's all right." That struck us as funny and we laughed and turned out the light.

As it turned out, this young man would not get an AIDS test on his own volition, despite numerous requests over a two-week period by both Cedar and finally me. I found out where he worked and wrote a letter to his employer explaining the situation, which seemed to encourage him. The test was performed; the results were mailed to me. Negative, thank God. Cedar was no longer seeing him anyway.

She wrote about this incident in her diary:

"That was one of those inexplicable things that I just did to do it. I had all sorts of odd considerations, like I wanted to lose my virginity at seventeen, because that's how old Gloria Swanson was when she did. Yes, Gloria Swanson. We're talking back in 1918 or so, here.

"We were acting in a movie together and having unprotected sex every night, and eventually I felt so low I thought I would die. When the filming ended and I saw my parents again because they had been out of town, I told my mother what I had done. I think it's the first and only time I have ever made her cry. I guess one thing I can say for myself is that I don't suffer from lack of candor."

The odds were that my daughter would have sex again without talking to me first. She admitted this herself. We finally had our talk about birth control and she promised she would use protection the next time.

But it took weeks for this raw wound between us to heal completely.

AN UNCOMMON LIFE

39

ROCKABILLY DANCING

Cedar flew in the door as I was taking up the evening meal, her favorite mixture of colored veggie noodles, nutritional yeast, butter and soy sauce. "Oh, no, broccoli!" she looked askance at the side dish. Ever since I'd bought some organic broccoli with aphids stuck to the trunk the month before, she would examine each miniature tree cross-eyed, searching for bugs.

"Why bother, they're already cooked anyway."

"Oh Mom, that's so gross," she stared at me, disgusted.

The filming for *In the Open* had wrapped, and on that Friday she had started a class at our church. She met a young woman there named Eva who invited her to go swing dancing that night.

"Eva is picking me up at eight. We're driving to Ybor City to some place where they give you lessons before the dance."

"That sounds like fun." She'd found a friend her own age! I was amazed.

Eva was there on time. She was a tall attractive blonde with tattoos circling her ankles just above a pair of green converse tennis shoes. This was her point of reality with Cedar, who wore the same exact brand and color. She was friendly and loose limbed, comfortable in her body. She grinned and shook my hand when Cedar introduced us.

"We'll be back around midnight, Mom. Don't worry about waiting up for me." Cedar and I kissed goodbye.

I did wait for Cedar to get home; I wanted to hear all about it, and of course I'd been worried all night. Ybor City was all the way on the far side of Tampa, over twenty miles away down two separate freeways.

Cedar breezed in at twelve-thirty. "Mom, it was so great!" She hadn't even shut the door yet.

"Shhh, Dad's asleep, let's go in your bedroom."

"I'm starving!" she replied in a stage whisper.

I fixed her a snack, applesauce with cinnamon and hot carob rice milk that we carried into her room. We sat on her bed, facing each other cross-legged as she ate.

"So what happened?" I asked.

"First of all, I really like Eva. We have so much in common. She's an artist, a singer. She just made a CD with her dad. That's the other thing; she's really close to her parents, too.

"We got there and a couple was giving lessons to the crowd—1940s style swing dancing. I caught on really fast and before the end of the night guys were asking me to dance. It was so much fun. It's nothing like what I've done but I have the idea I could really be good at it."

"That's great! Are you going again soon?"

"That's the thing—there's another dance tomorrow in Tampa and Eva can't make it. Do you think you could take me?"

The next night we drove there in our little blue Volvo, parking in the lot and walking up to the one-story building together.

There were people sitting at tables lining three sides of the floor and crowding the center dance floor, a mixture of clean-cut looking 'squares' of all ages and punk-greaser hybrids, mostly in their late 20s and early 30s. The punk-greaser men wore pompadours, earrings, white t-shirts and tight jeans. The women had ponytails or spiked short hair and wore vintage-looking clothes from the 1950s. Both sexes were decorated by tattoos in varying degrees of intensity. "Interesting," I said to Cedar as we slunk through the crowd to an unoccupied table.

The music being spun by the DJ for the current dance wasn't the relatively sedate big band sound of the 1940s. This was intense and fast paced—Jerry Lee Lewis belting out *Great Balls of Fire*. Before we made it to the table, a short stocky fellow with a black pompadour grabbed Cedar's hand and gave me a little grin. She was on the floor, following his lead, spun and turned, twisting her feet from side to side while they held hands at arm's length. On the last note of the song, Mike (that was his name, she introduced us later) leaned her backwards almost parallel to the floor and she didn't look the least bit alarmed.

She gave him a hug and looked around for where I sat. "Mom! That was great!" She was only slightly out of breath.

"That was amazing. Is this how you were dancing last night?"

"No, this is different. It's called rockabilly. It's faster paced, and the music is from the 1950s. I saw some kids dancing like this last night but it's the first time I've tried it."

The DJ played Carl Perkins, Elvis, Bo Diddley and several of the Big Band numbers. The straight people waited for *their* music before they got on the floor, but the Rockabillies danced them all.

I thought Cedar caught on awfully fast and was already dancing like the *bad girls* from 1956. When a stranger invited me to dance I laughed—it was the furthest thing from my mind. "No thank you, I'm just here to watch my daughter."

At midnight Cedar announced she was beat and said her goodbyes, hugs to at least five sweaty young men. "Did you have fun?' I asked unnecessarily.

"It was incredible."

The next morning she was making plans to go dancing again that night. "Brian is picking me up at eight-thirty. Do you remember meeting him?" I had a fuzzy recall of a tall man in his thirties with long curly hair.

"Is he the guy with the shoulder length hair?" I asked.

"Yes. He's a really good dancer and he asked me to go with him. He'll pick me up after dinner."

"Why don't you invite him to dinner? I'm making enchiladas." If she thought I was being nosy she didn't mention it. "Sure, I'll ask him."

Brian rang our doorbell at five-thirty, right on time.

"Mom, this is Brian."

"Hello." I held out my hand.

"Pleased to meet you," he said. He shook my hand and looked at the floor. A little shy, I thought.

We ate quietly in the kitchen. "This is really delicious," he said when I asked him if he'd like seconds. "But I'm stuffed." He seemed like a nice guy. My mom antenna didn't pick up any hidden intentions. Besides, Cedar had already told me he wasn't her type. Maybe it was the long hair; Cedar preferred her men shorn. She even complained to her father about his little pony tail.

They left for the dance, and when she got home after midnight Cedar assured me he'd been a perfect gentleman.

"We're going out again in a few days." Cedar looked radiant. "I love dancing, Mom. And I love all the guys in this group. They're definitely not your typical middle class young people."

Cedar had a hard time with the *mall crowd* kids. She told me "Around them I feel like I'm from Saturn."

"I know what you mean." I remembered my own teen years; a foreign presence in a high school full of kids headed for college, early marriage or Vietnam. I rebelled against my mother, who agreed with Time Magazine's "generation gap" and "hippie" platitudes.

"Just wait till you have kids," my mother told me with satisfaction, "you'll see what it's like." She had smiled sardonically.

But her words served to contrast my own mothering experience. Not given to praying, I often thanked whatever forces had aligned to give me this talented, loving and near-perfect daughter.

40

DRIVING LESSONS

Since age sixteen, Cedar had been asking for driving lessons. There was always something in the way—art shows, jewelry making, classes. The day after she turned seventeen, she cornered me.

"Mom, you've got to teach me. I hate having to depend on you and dad or my friends to take me everywhere." She was right, of course.

"Okay, you get your learner's permit and I'll take you out during the day."

She studied the booklet in one evening and got every question right when she took the test at the DMV the following day. "So let's go driving!" she said as soon as she and Ed walked in the door.

"I can't stop what I'm doing right now, but tomorrow morning I promise we'll do our first lesson."

Before lunch the next day we drove to an empty high school parking lot and switched seats. Cedar took the wheel of the Volvo and grinned at me. I said "OK, we'll do everything one step at a time."

"Mom, I'm ready!" she rolled her eyes.

We went through everything carefully, slowly. Which pedal is the brake, which one the gas, how to put it in first gear, easing it into motion.

She had a few frustrating frog hops going from first to second gear. But during that first lesson she had gotten it figured out and could drive smoothly all the way across the empty lot after only an hour's practice. We went back there for a few days, slowly easing out onto a relatively empty street by the third day. I felt like pinching myself. I was teaching my daughter to drive! Amazing. Ed had taught me to drive when I was 30 and pregnant with Cedar. *I'd* had no desire to learn until I was confronted with the prospect of handling two small children on the L.A. bus lines.

After a week Cedar had outgrown the sleepy streets near our apartment. It was time for real traffic. "Dad, you need to take me. Mom doesn't want to." It was true. I had visions of Cedar driving us down the freeway and me failing to make that instantaneous snap judgment that would have saved us both from a fiery car crash.

He started her on busy Highway 19, close to our apartment building. There were six lanes of traffic to deal with, but she did a good job, even making left turns on green lights (no arrows) with aplomb. I heard all about it when they got back an hour later.

After a few days more practice, Ed told me he was going to let her drive on 60 towards Tampa, then onto 275, the freeway.

"Are you sure she's ready for that?" the thought terrified me.

"Don't be such a worry wart," he said offhandedly. I scowled at him.

After two weeks of freeway driving, Cedar felt ready to take the test for her permanent license. Ed drove her to the DMV, about fifteen minutes away. When I heard the doorknob turn after an hour I looked up expectantly, thinking big grins and celebratory hugs. But Cedar pushed her way roughly past Ed and dashed to her room moaning "I'll never get my license!" She slammed her door with a dramatic rush of air. I heard the lock click.

"Cedar, talk to me!" I jiggled the handle.

"Go away!" she shouted, sobbing.

"Ed, what happened?" my tone was a little accusatory, which wasn't at all fair.

"She didn't make a full stop at a stop sign."

Laura called her a few minutes later to see if she had passed the test and through the door I could hear Cedar murmuring to her. She'd calmed down. When she opened her door she said "I'm sorry," and gave me a hug.

"That's okay, baby. We'll do some more driving and you can take the test again next week."

"Yeah?" she said tentatively.

"Sure. I didn't pass my driving test the first time either," I said, although that might not have been strictly true. Maybe I just *thought* I shouldn't have passed.

"You don't mind taking me out driving more?"

"Of course not! Besides, it'll give us more time to look for your new car."

Once she got her license, Cedar would be driving our Volvo, the safest car I knew of. But whenever we saw a tractor, golf cart or any other slow moving, ridiculous looking non-car semi-vehicle, I said, "that's what I'm buying you," to make her laugh.

The next week she took the test again and passed.

"Can I take the car to Laura's house tonight?" It was frightening, letting her drive off on her own that first time. But she was a good driver, and after a week I could even sit beside her without pressing on the ghost brake every time she slowed down.

41

The Doctor

Cedar was at the doctor for a checkup. Several physicians over the years had mentioned her heart murmur, always reassuring me it was minor. But occasional doctor's visits put my mind at ease.

Dr. J. listened to her chest carefully, moving the stethoscope around the whole area. "There's something here that should be checked out more closely," she told me, looking a little worried. Cedar got dressed and the doctor talked to me privately.

"She should get an echocardiogram. We have a technician who comes in once a week who can administer one. I think you should make an appointment."

"What do you think it is?" I asked her.

"It could be a valve that's not functioning properly. Those can be repaired. But I'm not really sure what's wrong. It's something more than just a murmur."

Oh my god! Surgery? I looked so distressed that the doctor gave me a hug. "Don't worry about it now. We'll get the echo done and see what we find out." I made an appointment for Thursday, three days away.

Cedar was sitting in the waiting room. I said, "Let's go home; we'll talk on the way."

Cedar seemed more annoyed than upset. "Why do I have to get this test?"

"Oh, the doctor just wants to check things out. She couldn't quite tell what was going on with the murmur and wants to make sure everything is okay," I said in what I hoped passed for a breezy sounding explanation.

I told Ed what happened at the doctor's. He was calm, said just get the test then we'll decide what to do.

Cedar had the echocardiogram on Thursday morning, and Dr. J. said she would call me as soon as she heard from the specialist who would be looking it over.

She called me Friday at ten in the morning.

"Merry, Cedar does have something wrong with her heart. It's a condition called hypertrophic cardiomyopathy, or HCM. The heart is pumping too hard and is quite enlarged. It's a serious condition."

"But what about the murmur?" I stammered.

"She has a heart murmur, but in this case it's a symptom of her condition. I'm afraid you'll have to become very good friends with a heart specialist." She spoke to me with a doctorly smile in her voice, as if convincing a child to take bad-tasting medicine.

"A heart specialist? What would a specialist do?"

"Cedar could die suddenly from HCM." She paused briefly, as if I could possibly take this in before she went on. "Her doctor may want to put her on medication. If that's the recommendation, be sure it's a drug that will affect her mentation the least."

"What's mentation?"

"Her ability to reason, her thinking process."

"Oh." I couldn't think of anything else to say. I was barely absorbing this nightmare with all its distinct and surprising horrors.

I thanked Dr. J. for calling and quietly hung up the phone. I sat on my bed and listened to a flock of Quaker parakeets squawking as they swooped over our apartment on their way to the oak tree. Ed had left for class an hour earlier and Cedar was still in bed Dr. J. had given me names of several heart specialists to call, so I dialed the first number on the list, Dr. H.'s office. When the receptionist answered, I explained why I was calling. "My daughter has just been diagnoscd with HCM." The acronym sounded foreign to me, but she knew exactly what I meant.

"Do you need the transplant division?" she asked. I had no idea what she was talking about. "Oh, perhaps she's not ready for that yet," her crisp reply to my stupefied silence. I thought maybe she didn't understand why I was calling after all, or maybe *transplant* had some meaning I didn't know about.

I tried another approach. "I just want to make an appointment for my daughter to get an evaluation."

She asked me how old Cedar was, did I have insurance, etc. Insurance. It just occurred to me that heart specialists were probably very expensive. And no, we didn't have medical insurance.

The crisp voice suggested I talk to a Florida organization that helped insure seriously ill children. I'd just copied down the number she gave me when I heard Cedar's bedroom door open. "Mom, what can I have for breakfast?" Cedar's sleepy voice. She'd been writing last night and it was early for her to be up.

"I'll be right there." I thanked the woman for her help and hung up.

I made her scrambled eggs and sat next to her at the kitchen table while she ate. "Cedar, the doctor called about the echocardiogram."

"So what do I have?" She made her voice a little sarcastic, hiding the worry.

"It's called," I stopped to read it off the paper where I had the doctor spell it out. "Hypertrophic cardiomyopathy."

"What's that?" she furrowed her brow.

"It's a heart condition, I don't know a lot about it. We're supposed to see a specialist."

"Oh, great." She looked annoyed, then burst into tears.

"Oh, sweetie," I held her awkwardly, hugging her sideways over her plate.

I was relieved when Cedar left to rehearse with the "Storytellers," a local group of actors who went to hospitals and schools to perform for children. Cedar was playing the blue fairy in *Sleeping Beauty*, which seemed like the perfect thing for her to be doing that day.

We had several art shows coming up and I was, as usual, low on all my best selling designs. "I should take a walk first," I thought, watching an egret glide toward the pond, settling lightly on the far bank.

In slow motion I picked up my favorite mug, one we traded for some of my jewelry at a recent art show. A brown lizard curved sinuously around the speckled brown base like a modern petroglyph, the handle built on with a comfortable thumbprint fitting. I felt its weight in my hand, seeing it with the after eyes of new context, overlaid with a film of potential tragedy. I held it close to my body, afraid of moving forward.

"I've got to get busy," I whispered to myself. I opened the door to a relentlessly blue Florida sky. Downstairs our neighbor, Don the retired Army Ranger, was feeding peanuts to the squirrels. He called them "tree rats."

"Good morning Don."

"That you, Merry?" Don was blind.

"Yeah. I'm going down to the office to get some coffee. Do you want a cup?"

"No, but thanks." Don was a man of few words.

I was walking slowly, feeling the earth under my feet, trying to rebalance. By the time Ed came home for lunch I felt as if I had been waiting for weeks to talk to him.

42

More Doctors

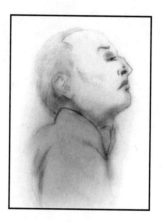

Dr. L. walked into the room and shut the door. He was a short man with sharp features and thin arms covered with dark hair. He looked over the results of the EKG and echocardiogram just ordered for Cedar and frowned. "Her condition is very serious. Frankly I'm surprised there aren't more outward signs of her disease." He stared at Cedar, appraising her. "She looks quite normal. Many children who have a heart condition as devastating as hers have other deformities as well." He addressed all his comments to Ed and me.

"Is she involved with any strenuous sports?"

"No, but she's a dancer. You know, you *can* talk to her."

He ignored that. "She'll have to stop. It's very dangerous for her to be doing anything where she could get out of breath." He spoke briskly, in a voice that brokered no contradiction.

I glanced at Cedar sidelong, afraid of the effect this horrid man must be having on her. She stared straight ahead, frowning.

Dr. L. strode quickly and importantly from the room clutching his clipboard with his left hand. I followed him out and walked straight to the receptionist's desk. "Is there another doctor we can see?"

"Is there a problem?" she asked, bored.

"Yes. I don't want to deal with that doctor again." I was furious. How could such an insensitive blockhead be a pediatric cardiologist?

She told me there was another doctor, Dr. P. who could see us if we wanted to wait. We ate lunch nearby and returned an hour later.

Dr. P. was a tall man with horn-rimmed glasses, a little soft in the middle which made him seem kindly and approachable even before he spoke. He introduced himself to our family, shaking our hands warmly. "Cedar, could you hop up on the examining table?" he listened to her heart, gently moving the stethoscope underneath the hospital gown, stopping here and there to listen.

He spoke quietly. "Cedar, you do have hypertrophic cardiomyopathy." He pulled out some charts and showed us where her heart muscle had thickened. "The muscle has gotten larger because your heart has to work harder to pump the blood."

"It's often a genetic condition, but it doesn't look like anyone else in your family had HCM." He had obviously read the paperwork we filled out. My mom had always bragged about the health of the Whitaker clan. For generations the whole hale and hearty bunch sprang forth without a single congenital defect. Ed's family had the usual late middle-age heart trouble, but nothing related to this.

"There *is* a real danger of sudden death. We can prescribe medicine which will ease the symptoms, but it seems you are asymptomatic right now anyway." He made it clear that the medicine would do nothing to stop a fatal occurrence, as he called it.

"Is there anything natural she could take that would help?" I asked.

He told us about the possible benefits of CO-Q 10 and vitamin E. He approved of some therapeutic massage and said Chiropractic adjustments would be acceptable. "Anything that makes her feel better is fine," he said.

"What about dancing?" Cedar asked him.

"That should be okay. If you get out of breath or have any pain, then stop immediately."

He wanted her to wear a halter monitor for 24 hours to measure any intermittent arrhythmias. She was sent off to get fitted with little round electrodes, fastened to her chest with white tape. The monitor would be worn over her shoulder on a strap like a tiny pocketbook.

While she was gone, I asked Dr. P. what her prognosis was. He told me that her condition was "very serious," and that she could be a candidate for a heart transplant in the near future.

"What's the oldest someone with her condition could hope to live?" I asked shakily.

"Maybe into her late forties, even with a transplant. If she lives into her thirties, she'll start to experience congestive heart failure."

The doctor may have been soft-spoken and sensitive, but I wanted to grab him by his lapels and yell, "You don't know who this is! Cedar is remarkable, talented and important. This can't *possibly* be true!" Instead I broke into tears, covering my face. He silently handed me a box of tissue.

When Cedar returned she got some last minute instructions from the doctor about wearing the monitor and he handed us a print-out about HCM. It was a four page Xeroxed sheet that explained the condition with diagrams and frequently asked questions. Then he told us to set our next appointment and we all shook hands.

Cedar was quiet on the drive home. I turned around to look at her.

"Are you okay?"

"Oh yeah, I'm just great." She was sitting in the back seat of the Volvo, her long legs curled under her, staring out the window.

"Cedar, remember doctors don't know everything." It was the only thing I could come up with and besides I knew it had some basic truth.

She thought about this for a while.

Then, "Yeah, why should I agree with someone who thinks I could suddenly *die*?" She sat up straighter, a little mad. "That's insane."

By the time we got home Cedar was complaining about the halter monitor and refused to leave the house until the twenty four hours were up. "It's way too embarrassing to wear in public," she assured me.

Ed drove to the library and borrowed five classic films, all comedies, and the three of us watched Laurel and Hardy's *Way out West* after a home made pizza dinner, laughing at those two derby-topped clowns bumbling through their version of a western. We had root beer floats for dessert.

I sat on Cedar's bed after she'd brushed her teeth and we talked about the doctor's visit.

"It's so unfair," she held my hand. "My life is just getting started." She wasn't sobbing out loud, but wiped a tear away.

"Look Sweetie, we can handle this. And doctors really don't know everything," I reminded her again.

"Mommy, I love you." I kissed her warm cheek and tucked her blankets in.

"Tell me a story," she said.

Years ago I made up stories for David and Cedar before they went to sleep, usually about a miniature dragon that flew around the house with a friend, an even tinier fairy. "I'm a little out of practice," I told her.

"I don't care," she said.

I closed my eyes, trying to come up with something.

"Well, this tiny purple dragon came in the little girl's room, landing on the curtain rod and whistling. That was how he communicated, by whistling. One day he couldn't find the curtain rod and he…." I was at a loss.

"Oh, Mommy," she laughed. "It's okay." She reached up with her slender arms and pulled me down in a pillow-smothering embrace. I turned my head sideways so I could breathe.

"I love you, Baby. Get a good night's sleep and tomorrow we'll do something fun." I kissed her again and turned off the light.

43

Plays

Cedar had a part in a St. Petersburg Little Theatre production of *Witness for the Prosecution*. She played the sexy young typist to Sir Wilfred, the lawyer for the defense. For this part she worked on an East London cockney accent, rewinding and replaying a demo tape Mandy had made for her.

Cedar had been cast shortly before all the medical business had begun. Before the play even opened, she had a second appointment to see Dr. P. so she could return the halter monitor and get the results, which were inconclusive. Cedar was behind the wheel that time, and joked "You and Dad are going to need the heart treatment after letting me drive through all this traffic."

During the office visit she asked Dr. P "Would you like to see the play?"

"I'd love to. Tell me when it is and I'll try to make it."

Cedar became friends with the woman who played the female lead of Christine Helm. This actress had been a singer for Benny Goodman in the 1940s. With a little prompting from Cedar she told her all about life on the road with the sometimes tyrannical band leader.

I drove to St Petersburg to watch the play with my old friend Nancy and her youngest daughter, Katherine. Her older child, Diana, was in college in West Virginia, studying philosophy and theatre. Nancy is a former nurse, and one of the first people I told when I found out Cedar had HCM. Nancy, small, quiet and understanding knew exactly what it was, which was strangely comforting.

Nancy had never seen Cedar perform, which made the evening especially delectable. I could hardly wait for Cedar to make her entrance, which didn't take long— she was in the very first scene.

"Shall I make the tea, Mr. Carter?" She flounced into the room, her navy skirt with white polka dots swinging flirtatiously around her calves. After delivering the line she peered closely at her nails.

"It's hardly time yet, Greta."

"It is by my watch," she replied offhandedly.

It was a real character part. Greta was a slightly stupid girl full of self-important opinions which she spewed unbidden to Sir Wilfred. Cedar was in her element.

We drove home afterwards, Cedar sharing the back seat with quiet Katherine. She was still flushed and bubbly from her performance. "Did you like the play?" she asked Nancy.

"Cedar, you were wonderful!" Nancy's eyes were shining.

When *Witness* wrapped, Cedar started rehearsals for *The Importance of being Earnest.*

She was Cecily Cardew, the young heiress who falls in love with Algernon, a young scoundrel pretending the identity of Ernest, the product of his friend Jack's imagination. This Oscar Wilde Victorian comedy of errors was right up Cedar's alley. She made good friends with her co-star, who played Gwendolyn, the other love interest.

But the man Cecily loved tried to French kiss Cedar during their scenes together. "Mom, what should I do?"

"You could bite his tongue," I suggested.

She didn't but she threatened to, which seemed to work nicely.

By this time Cedar had changed her last name to Bennett, thinking Rosenfield might cause typecasting. The program for *Earnest* was the first time her new name appeared in print.

The Wild Hearts continued to perform their improvisational comedy at a local coffeehouse called *Mother's Milk*, a re-invented gas station north of downtown Clearwater. I only went one time, but remember clearly their clever originations and instant rejoinders.

"How do you think of something that's actually funny when you're under pressure?" I asked her afterwards.

"It's actually pretty easy. Plus I'm with my friends, and we sort of have a rhythm going," she told me.

Cedar discovered P.G. Wodehouse after stumbling across the *Jeeves and Wooster* videos from Britain in the Clearwater library. They starred Hugh Laurie as the bumbling Bertie Wooster and Stephen Fry as the level-headed butler Jeeves. It had been a TV series in Great Britain in the early 1990s, set in the deco years of the 1920s and 1930s, Cedar's favorite time period. "They are *so* funny!" Bertie's inept self importance was the best part, sending her into breath-taking guffaws of laughter.

We found four or five episodes in the library and kept our eyes open for more. I gave Cedar *The Jeeves Collection*, P.G. Wodehouse's three novels about this pair, for Christmas that year. She read them straight through, with a dictionary so she could translate the language of that more literate time. Her laughter spilled through the closed bedroom door. "Mom, listen to this…" she shouted, unable to keep a passage to herself.

Cedar did the same things she loved to do before we found out about her renegade heart, and the only time she even mentioned it was when we had doctor appointments, every few months.

But the knowledge of her condition and the danger she was in followed me around like a grey shadow. For several weeks after our first appointment with Dr. P., I watched white-haired old ladies wistfully, sometimes blinking back tears. Without a medical miracle she wouldn't even reach her fifties. Dr. P. had given us a little hope; he thought unraveling the cause of HCM was about five years in the future. I couldn't guess what that might mean for our daughter.

Cedar rarely acknowledged this blight on her happiness and I never told her what Dr. P. had said about her abbreviated future. Past that fateful doctor's visit, the possibility of death wasn't even acknowledged by Cedar. She liked comedies; her life ending suddenly was too much like an ill-written melodrama. I can hear her voice, "It wouldn't make sense. The author wasn't working hard enough to tie all the loose ends together and took the easy way out by letting her die."

AN UNCOMMON LIFE

44

THE BOYFRIEND

Cedar still went dancing every Friday night. Afterwards she'd tell me about the inter-dance intrigues; rockabilly dancers versus swing dancers (the rockabilly "kids" were the cool ones), inconstant lovers, the latest tattoos, various crushes. Cedar had her share of those from love-sick men. One fellow tried to impress Cedar by telling her all his friends called him "The Knife." But Cedar told me behind his back they called him "The Spork."

After one of her nights out she told me about an interesting young man with the unlikely name of Cosmo. He impressed Cedar not only for his ability to never shut up, but also because of the enormous number of tattoos he had. "His arms are covered all the way up to his knuckles," she told me in mock awe.

She found it amusing that these guys saved up their hard earned money to pay for tattoos. "Not only are they very expensive; but when they're old and flabby those tattoos will look awful!" she said to me, shaking her head.

A week later Cedar told me she had a date with Cosmo, which surprised me. "What are you planning to do?" I asked suspiciously.

"Mom, it's okay. We're just going to get something to eat after the dance."

Two weeks and several more dates went by and I decided it was time for Ed and me to meet this character. Cedar told us he was partial to Italian food. We had just read about an authentic Italian restaurant that recently opened on Highway 19 so we called for reservations.

Cosmo showed up at our door twenty minutes late. He was a large man with gigantic hands tattooed all the way to the knuckles, as Cedar had warned. His red hair was completely slicked back, and there were tattoos up above his shirt surrounding his neck like a satanic lace collar. When he smiled, a gold tooth gleamed in front.

"Nice to meet you," he mumbled, shuffling around in the space right inside the door. His eyes shifted, guiltily I thought, from Ed to me. He also looked like he thought this dinner idea was stupid.

During the five mile drive, Cedar and Cosmo sat in the back seat holding hands. I craned my head around and asked him what he did for a living. I was trying hard not to stare at his arms. But I can't remember a thing he said, not even well enough to piece together a conversation.

The restaurant was in a strip mall with Italian vineyard scenes painted on the walls. Ed ordered antipasto for an appetizer and I looked forward to a big plate of grilled veggies, fresh mozzarella balls and tasty oblong olives with pits. At least, I thought, we'd have some delicious food.

What the waitress brought was a gigantic platter of meat slices tucked into interesting little shapes; origami ham and salami surrounded by inedible lacy greens, possibly raw collard. Cosmo helped himself heartily. It was a good thing too, because our entire family was vegetarian at the time.

He was dabbing at some blood on his arm with a little piece of tissue. "Did you hurt yourself?" I asked.

"Oh, it's nothing. I cut myself shaving."

He shaves his arms. It dawned on me. *He shaves his arms so you can see the tattoos.* After driving home I invited Cosmo upstairs for cheesecake, trying to be congenial. "This is really good, Mom." Cedar scraped her plate clean with her fork.

"Thanks Honey."

Cosmo looked at me and said, "That wasn't bad."

Cedar walked him to his car and didn't come back for an hour. "Do you think they went someplace?" I asked Ed.

"No, I think Cedar would've told us first." When the doorknob finally turned, I jumped.

"Is everything OK?" I asked Cedar.

Her face was flushed and she said, "Sure, why?" She spoke a little too offhandedly so I followed her to her room.

"What's going on?"

"Oh mom, Cosmo and I were making out in his car."

"I see. Are you sleeping with him?" I got right to the point.

"Yes, but we're using protection."

"Cedar, this man is almost seven years older than you. How much do you know about him?"

Cedar told me he was sweet with her and she felt protected by him. They had the rockabilly thing in common, although he never danced. I wondered how long this could possibly last.

When they broke up about two weeks later, Cedar wrote a few thoughts about him in her journal:

"By far my biggest SNAFU was ever getting involved with a certain character named Cosmo Moretti. I met him at a rockabilly show in Orlando when I was eighteen. I'd seen him a lot and obviously remembered him because you don't easily forget somebody who looks like that. He's tall

and slim with an enormous head that cannot go unnoticed. He has a gold tooth in front; both ears pierced, and he greases his hair back like a 1930s gangster. He has tattoos that all but cover his arms and hands...and neck!

"I think any normal person would have found him, if not out-right offensive to the eye, at least undesirable as a boyfriend. But yours truly has got some mighty strange taste in boys."

45

THE CALL

In August of 2000, Ed and I made a trip to California to do an art show and visit Terry and Rick. I remember absolutely nothing about the show, but the visit to Terry's was heart wrenching. The cancer was marching through her body, wearing down her troops of T-cells like a renegade militia.

She was wispy-thin and looked about ten years older. I hugged her gently but was still worried I'd crack a rib.

We sat in their living room, eating pizza and talking. "She's skinny, huh?" Rick pointing out the obvious, breaking through our awkwardness. He encouraged her to eat, trying to fatten her up with pepperoni and cheese.

After dinner Terry and I talked in the kitchen. She wanted to make me a cup of tea. "I'm not afraid," she told me. I searched for something encouraging or funny or intelligent to say.

"What does the doctor think?" I asked her, realizing too late this was the worst possible question.

"There's nothing more he can do. Now I'm just worried about the pain. I don't want it to hurt."

Before, when Terry and I planned grandchildren, fantasy trips to Yosemite, selling our artwork and growing old together it was the two of us. Her cancer was behind bars, menacing but contained. I still wasn't sure how to approach this unleashed thing.

Terry was tired. She made us each a cup of tea and then had to lie down. I followed her into the bedroom.

"Are you able to eat more? It seems like you'd have more strength."

"I can't keep up with it. The cancer increases my metabolism so much that anything I eat gets used up immediately. Besides, I'm not really hungry." She could barely keep her eyes open now.

I kissed Terry on the forehead and walked quietly from the room.

When we got back to Florida I talked to Terry every other day. She was no longer working. Rick had taken over her freelance job as a securities analyst to pay the bills.

"The chemo makes me so tired," she'd complain to me. "I've lost all my hair, everywhere except for my legs and armpits. Of course," she said, chagrined.

"Do you have a wig?"

"No, they're too itchy. I just tie on a scarf. It's obvious I'm a cancer victim now and I hate that."

"Why don't you just go bald? That could be quite avant-garde."

"I have the wrong shaped head for that," she assured me. "I look like E.T."

"Oh, Terry—I can't believe two of my favorite women in the entire world are ill." I thought about the jewel-toned painting my brother Alex had done of Terry sitting cross legged on the beach with long-legged, eight-year-old Cedar sprawled in her lap. Alex had shown it to me the last time I'd visited New York for a show—it hung in the stairwell of his old Victorian home in Brooklyn.

"Do you have a slide of it I can show to Terry?" I'd asked him, knowing how much she would have loved it.

"Sure, somewhere here. Just remind me and I'll dig it up before you leave." But we'd both forgotten.

Terry was positive Cedar would survive. "Oh Mer, Don't worry about Cedar. I know she'll be fine." It was unreal to Terry that my beautiful nineteen-year-old daughter was also fighting for life.

Terry told me about Sue, Peter's new girlfriend. He and his wife had split up several months earlier, another source of distress for Terry. "I really like Sue. I've only met her once when I invited them over for dinner before I got so sick. She was down to earth and seemed so fond of Peter." I was glad he'd found love during this terrible time.

In September, Terry called me and said her vision had gotten blurry. She thought she needed new glasses but her optometrist found nothing wrong with her eyes. He suggested she see her oncologist, who discovered the cancer had reached her brain. He wanted to put a permanent shunt in her head to pour the chemo drugs directly on the tumor, a final degradation.

"Oh Terry, I'm so sorry."

She had her surgery a few days later. In the afternoon for us, her California morning, Terry called to say goodbye. The phone rang just after lunch.

"Hi Mer. Do you have some time to talk?" I had to listen carefully to her words, which were a little slurred.

"Of course I do."

"We had some good times together, didn't we?" Her voice was tired but cheerful, remembering. She laughed weakly, reminding me of a rare morning we went shopping together in San Francisco years earlier. She had left the Nordstrom's restroom trailing a line of toilet paper on her shoe, all the way back to the lady's dress department. I was sitting on our bed, cradling the phone, and trying not to let grief slip into my laughter.

"We had fun."

"You're really my sister," she said, "I love you so much."

I took a deep breath.

"I love you too. And you'll always be my sister." I had to clench my fist to keep from crying, but when we said goodbye I'd shed no audible tears. She asked to speak to Cedar.

They talked for a couple of minutes, but when Cedar passed the phone to Ed she looked puzzled. "Terry sounded sort of odd."

"She's just come out of surgery. She's still got those drugs affecting her," I replied, my hand over my mouth to keep grief contained.

"Mom, what's wrong?" Cedar was alarmed.

"Terry's very sick. I'm just worried about her." I didn't talk about Terry's cancer to Cedar anymore.

Cedar put her arm around me. "She'll be OK. She always seems to pull through."

"You're probably right," I said and hugged her.

46

GOODBYE

October of 2000 was a busy month. I had a show in Cincinnati and was staying with my eighty-year-old mom in Alexandria Kentucky, just across the river. She lived in her own little mother-in-law apartment attached to my brother and his wife's home by a shared laundry room. Kathryn Hutton had finally retired as an artist after sixty-five years of designing greeting cards and illustrating children's books.

Five years earlier, her blindness from macular degeneration became nearly complete. She could view things peripherally, but told me my face was just a shadow to her. But she imagined colors and designs complete with wide screen Technicolor hallucinations.

My sister Holly lived in Rhode Island and spoke to Mom every couple weeks. She and I debated whether this was a matter for concern. "But Mom is so *entertained* by her visions," Holly and I laughed.

Mom called me one early Saturday in July. "This morning I saw a gang of kids riding a sled across the lawn. They were dressed in clothing from the 1800s and the colors were just vivid!" She knew none of this was real, but she was completely undisturbed by it.

"Just don't mention it to the neighbors," I warned her, laughing.

Mom's apartment was painted white, original art filled one living room wall from the mid eye level almost to the floor. There was a mobile reminiscent of a Miró painting hanging in the middle of the room, next to an exuberant green and white striped spider plant with at least fifteen unruly babies escaping on runners.

She had a studio set up next to her kitchen where an unfinished painting of emerald woods sat on her easel, daubed at unenthusiastically every few months. Fed up with her inability to see well, interest in her own art had faded. "Mom, it really is beautiful. You should finish it," I encouraged her.

"Ahh..." she said, her words trailing off in self-disgust.

Mom had, as they say, excellent taste in everything and was absolutely and sometimes loudly impatient with *bad art*. This created some embarrassing moments, like the time my long-suffering brother Jeff took her to an exhibit of visually impaired artists' work. Mom planted her sturdy, now 4 feet 11 inch frame in front of one woman's painting, fisted hands placed defiantly on each hip. She shook her head in exaggerated dismay and said loud enough to be heard throughout the roomful of reverent patrons, "Good-Night, this is just *awful*!"

Jeff told me later, a crooked smile on his face, "The puzzle was whether or not she could even see it."

When I got back from the first day of my show, Vivaldi was blasting on Mom's CD player and she was on the phone, pretending she could hear the person on the other end of the line. She wore expensive hearing aids, but half the time they were on the blink completely, or shrieking loudly enough to be heard in the next room. "I'm sorry, you have the wrong number." She sounded annoyed and hung up.

"What did they say?"

"It was some man. I couldn't understand him too well because he mumbled." To my mother, all men mumbled. She had a difficult time hearing sounds in a low register.

The phone rang again. "I'll get it. Hello?"

"Merry, this is Rick. I just tried to call but your mom hung up on me!"

"Sorry. She doesn't hear well." I made sure she wasn't nearby. "How is Terry doing?"

I hadn't talked to her since her surgery two weeks earlier. She didn't want to talk to or see anyone but Rick, who took care of her tenderly. He bathed her and fed her hot dogs and Oreo cookies, the only things she wanted to eat.

"Mer, she passed away this morning."

Rick described the passing of his darling Terry, who slipped away as he held her in his arms. I started to cry, then Rick was sobbing, and it was no longer much of a conversation—just the two of us weeping over the thousands of miles from Kentucky to California.

Finally, "How's Peter doing?"

"He's okay. Maybe you should have Ed call him."

"Sure, I'll be talking to him tonight." I told Rick I loved him, and that we'd be seeing him before too long. "Call me anytime you need to talk."

"Nah, your mom will just hang up on me again." We laughed.

"Who was that?" Mom asked, concerned. She knew about my best friend being ill. I told her Rick called to tell me Terry had died that morning. I started to cry again, and her face contorted. She made grieving sounds, tears streaming as she sobbed for the death of a woman she had never met.

We held each other for a while, then Mom asked me if I'd like a cup of ginger tea. She disappeared into her bedroom while the water boiled, searching for something in her jewelry box.

"I thought you would appreciate this." She handed me a quote from a Rosamunde Pilcher book, one she had copied by hand to be read at her own funeral. It was beautiful, with truths about death not being so final a thing, more like stepping into the next room.

A week later, when Ed and I were home again, we made plans to fly to San Francisco for the funeral, just the two of us. Rick wanted to have music at the memorial service, and asked me to play my dulcimer and sing a song.

"I don't know if I can!" I said.

"It would mean a lot to Terry," he pointed out. "You know she'll be there."

Rick would be singing and playing, as well as his good friend, "Mr. Music," who was going to perform that Bob Dylan song with the line "She's got everything she needs, she's an artist, she don't look back."

It was a beautiful service, in the old building down on Market Street where Terry had done some Scientology classes. When I sang, I imagined her in the back of the room, smiling and relieved at last.

47

GLAD RAGS

Cedar was working on a screenplay set in her favorite time period, the Roaring 20s. This was the current project keeping her up until the wee hours. She called her film *Glad Rags*, which was slang for the stepping-out clothes worn by flappers.

It was a screwball comedy, one I could picture these actors in, back when they were young and fresh-faced—Fred Astaire, Cary Grant, Katharine Hepburn and Ginger Rogers. Cedar wrote the lead for herself, the Hepburn part. In the screen play, her name was Elsa, and her profession was scenario writer for silent films.

Her script started and ended with a black and white silent bit, to be filmed sort of choppy looking like the old classic movies before they had sound. Here's her description of the beginning:

"Elsa Babcock, young, vivacious, skips into frame in a chic bathing suit carrying a parasol. A remarkably endearing wise guy named Charlie Newcastle romps about with her. He shows her how to pose cheesecake for the camera; her knees bent and rear protruding.

"Charlie stands back to admire his handiwork. He seizes the opportunity and smacks her vulnerable rear end. She straightens up, stomps on his foot and makes a quick getaway behind the camera. He tries to coax her back."

For another five minutes or so, new characters enter the fray until the last part of the opening credits, when Elsa shows off by doing the splits.

"The others applaud her. Soon she realizes she can't get up. Fritz and Charlie take her arms and attempt to pull her up. On the third try they succeed with such force that they all topple over in a big clump."

And now the actual movie begins. She wanted it filmed in faded color, with titles appearing throughout the movie just like in the old silent films, even though this film was not meant to be silent.

I read the script again recently for the first time in many years, laughing without crying this time.

Back in 2000, Mandy read it and told Cedar she should enter it in a new contest HBO was sponsoring. It was called

Project Greenlight. The winner of the contest would get his or her script produced and aired on the cable station.

First Cedar had to convert her screenplay from the handwritten yellow tablets to the computer. When we lived in Rough and Ready she had taught herself how to type which was a very good thing.

In 2000, we still had no computer of our own, so Cedar spent a week learning how to use Laura's. Wayne and Laura hovered and helped her get going and she typed the entire script in a few days.

It was sent off, along with an information sheet about the author.

When asked the question of what her most significant personal issue was, this is what she said:

"I feel much older than I am, and it can be hard to get others to understand this sometimes, and not view me like a typical teenager."

Asked what makes her really angry, she said:

"People who condone racism and religious intolerance."

The question about what a best friend would think was her worst trait had this reply:

"I'm opinionated about what I don't like."

This is her response to the question asking what made her want to write a screen play:

"It's extremely rewarding for me to watch a film with enough creativity and humor in it to leave me feeling inspired. When I first saw classic films from the 1930s, this is exactly what they did for me. I realized how clever a screen play can be, and I wanted to see what I was capable of writing."

It was pleasant tension waiting for a response from the project. Cedar received a letter about six weeks later:

"Congratulations! You have been selected as eligible to advance to the Top 250 Round of the Project Greenlight Contest! Your fellow Contestants and Reviewers have read and reviewed your script, and based on their reviews as processed by the scoring system described in the Official Rules, your Submission was rated one of the top 250 screenplays in the entire contest. We received over 7,000 eligible scripts in total, so no matter what happens in this round or future rounds of the contest, you should feel incredibly proud of this achievement - keep on writing and pursuing your dreams!"

Cedar and I danced around the living room, laughing and hugging. "Baby, that's fantastic! You are amazing."

Cedar said, "I can't believe it! I'm so happy!" She received a copy of the primary review with comments. It was from someone who wasn't even fond of movies from that period and conceded that her script kept him interested until the very end.

For the next phase of the contest she had to submit a video of herself, three minutes or less in length, that would convey to the judges a *"sense of your talent and creativity."*

She and Wayne spent most of one afternoon shooting it in a bucolic setting near Laura's house. This is how Mandy described the first version they made:

"Wayne and Cedar came in the room and with completely straight faces said they thought they had the perfect video. 'Mandy, we want your opinion just to make sure,' Wayne said to me. The video started out with Cedar removing her coat slowly, one shoulder at a time as if she were a stripper. She spoke suggestively, licking her upper lip with her tongue and staring at the camera as if she were trying to seduce the judges. I wasn't sure what to say. I didn't want to hurt their feelings but this was definitely weird. I worried what Cedar's parents would think. I have got to say something, I remember thinking. When I finally turned around to comment, both of them were about to burst with laughter. They'd meant it as a joke and I'd completely fallen for it."

In the video actually sent to Greenlight, Cedar is walking along a trail, speaking about her favorite filmmaker, Buster Keaton. She's wearing her little winter coat, a fake leather one with a soft fur collar. Her face and body, barely adult, move gracefully while she explains herself, slim hands punctuating her words. When she smiles, the soft colors remind me of a living Vermeer painting.

She submitted the video, but someone else won the contest. It doesn't matter now. We have the film of Cedar talking about herself, our living portrait of her moment.

48

TEXAS CHRISTMAS

Since 1998, we've spent the two weeks leading up to Christmas, Christmas Eve included, selling my jewelry in Austin, Texas. This is a down home, Texas-style art show called "The Armadillo Bazaar," with live music every single night. Ray Wiley Hubbard (who wrote the popular song *Redneck Mother* in the '70s) performs, so does boogie-woogie piano player Marcia Ball, Texas-swing musician Ray Benson of *Asleep at the Wheel* and so on. Not all the musicians are famous, but they're all good.

We have made some dear friends among the eccentric artists, including Pat and Suzanne who make monsters for a living. They call their business *The Bungled Jungle*, and concoct creatures from latex, wire, old goat wool, bright colored paint and God knows what else. They attract all kinds of people to their booth—guys in three piece suits, second-generation hippies, young women with babies. Both she and Pat tell their customers the most outrageous things in calm, serious voices. They warn them against particularly sneaky or vicious monsters, giving them advice on their care and what to do if they get bitten. Most of their customers laugh, but I've seen some people look at the two of them with wide eyes and open-mouthed astonishment.

Our other favorites are Ann and Derek. Ann is over 6 feet tall, slim and delicately boned. She wears sparkly glasses from the 1950s that taper to little points above her cheekbones. Derek is a large, burly man with a full beard who sometimes wears his long hair in a bun held up with chopsticks. Ann does life castings of people, their faces and sometimes their entire (nude) bodies. She adds lovely details to the final polished work—gently painted features and little flower crowns make them look like they've stepped out of a fairy tale, transformed into fine porcelain. Her other products include vintage ties for men that she hand paints with cheesecake 1940s women. Derek often wears a fat burgundy tie with a naked seductress, her nipples modestly hidden behind a tie bar.

The first two years we were there, I flew home on December twenty-first, four days before the show ended. In 1999, Cedar picked me up at the airport.

"I wish we could cut down our own Christmas tree like we used to in the Santa Cruz Mountains," Cedar reminisced on the way home.

"I think Home Depot will have to do," I sighed.

We drove there from the airport, discovering they had a stack of still-green trees outside the glass doors.

"How's this one look?" Cedar had picked out the bushiest, greenest one of the bunch, and the most expensive.

"Pretty good, but how about this one?" I held the price tag out for her to see.

"Even better," she laughed.

We hauled our modestly-sized evergreen up the stairs to our apartment, balancing it in the red metal stand and trimming it while Leon Redbone crooned carols from the CD player.

"How about some hot chocolate?" she asked.

"Don't you think we should turn up the air conditioning and pretend it's actually cold first?"

"Are you serious?"

"No. Your dad would kill us."

A year later, in the winter of 2000, we decided to drive to Austin and fly Cedar out there to join us a few days before the show ended. She had only seen Texas through the windows of our Ryder truck, zooming through at 70 mph in 1998, and had never been to Austin.

I couldn't wait for my friends to meet Cedar, whom I'd been bragging about for two years. I had been telling anyone who would listen that Cedar was "more talented than I am," which I firmly believed was true.

I had a surprise for Cedar, a Christmas tree decorated and lit right in front of the window of our motel room. I sat in the lobby and waited for her and Ed to arrive from the airport. Half the artists, myself included, had come down with the flu the week before. But I had barely, and thankfully, recovered.

Cedar approached me through the motel double doors with a cranberry-lipsticked smile, wearing a bandana backwards on her head, arms out to for a hug. "Baby Girl!" we both shouted at once. We were used to curious stares, and ignored the other hotel guests as we rushed into each other's arms.

The next day, Cedar, Suzanne and I spent a few girly hours shopping at second-hand shops in Austin while our men manned the booths. Cedar was in vintage heaven, uncovering a red cotton jacket with "Emily" embroidered across the front, a short sleeved shirt with a giraffe appliqué on front, and scads of dresses from the '50s and '60s that fit her slim frame perfectly. I think I spent over two hundred dollars, which was an amazing amount for thrift store shopping.

For the last three days of the show Cedar stayed in the motel during the day, working on her newest screenplay. When I came back to make dinner in our kitchenette, we ate in our room, then drove to the Bazaar together with Ed's meal in a paper bag.

Cedar and I stood behind the counter in our booth, talking about her day's writing while Ed ate his brown rice and veggies in the artist's storage room upstairs. She said, "It's going really well. I think it's just as funny as *Glad Rags* and I'm having a great time with the dialogue."

"That's wonderful, Sweetie. I can't wait to read it."

The musicians were setting up on the stage, sound tests with teasing bits of guitar and voice were sent out over the PA system. "Mom, did you hear that? It sounds like Texas Swing!"

An hour later the band lit into their first number with energetic vengeance and to my ears a rockabilly beat. Cedar was now directly behind the metal folding chairs where everybody else sat and listened, dancing with a young man she'd just met. I watched them for a while. That year the stage was just forward a couple rows from our booth, the chairs extended back and ended where I could barely see the concrete dance floor if I stretched my neck way out.

Customers were showing up. "Is this your booth?"

"Oh, sorry, yes. I was watching my daughter dance."

"Great music tonight!" they shouted. It could get pretty loud. But that night I didn't mind.

49

TOWARDS HOME

The Armadillo Christmas Bazaar ended at eleven p.m. December 24, 2000, after the last band played their final song. The *anthem* was queued up again, the song that every shopping day opened and closed with—*I Wanna Go Home with the Armadillo,* recorded by Jerry Jeff Walker sometime in the 1970s.

Cedar helped us take down our booth. She carefully packed away the rows of unsold jewelry on their cards in green plastic containers with lids, unstrung the holiday tinsel from the poles and swept off the rug so we could roll it up and stow it in the van. I was exhausted, but Cedar, the night owl, was wide awake. "Come on Mom, we need to finish so we can play all day tomorrow!"

We got back to our room at two-thirty in the morning. "I think we need a cup of hot cocoa and some brie before we go to sleep," she suggested.

So we celebrated with a private Christmas Eve party. We watched the last part of *Holiday Inn* with Bing Crosby and Fred Astaire on Turner Classic Movies, slurping hot chocolate and brushing cracker crumbs from our sheets.

Cedar woke up around nine o'clock, late for Christmas morning but early for us, considering. I popped frozen waffles in the toaster for drenching with maple syrup and butter, then dialed David's number in California. "Did you get your box of goodies?"

"Yes, thanks, Mom. I shared it with my roommates."

"How many do you have now?"

"Six."

"Jeez!"

Cedar and David wished each other Merry Christmas. It had been four years since they had been together, I thought with an uncomfortable pang. They were joking about something and Cedar called him "Day-Dee" her toddler era word evolved into a pet name over the years.

I felt tears quivering on the edge of overflow and I wiped them away before she hung up.

"Is something the matter, Mom?"

"Oh, you know me. I'm just a little extra sentimental this time of year."

"I miss David, too." She hugged me.

Ed was sitting on the bed, eyeing the packages. "Shall we unwrap presents?"

I had a special gift for Cedar that I had tricked her into picking up for me in Clearwater at our church bookstore. I had it wrapped ahead of time and led her to believe it was for Ed. So when I handed her the foil-wrapped box, she looked at me suspiciously.

"Yeah, it *is* Ed's but I want you to unwrap it for him. You'll see, it's better that way," I grinned at her, knowing I made absolutely no sense.

She tore off the paper, opened the box and gave a little gasp. "Oh, Mommy! I can't believe you got this for me!" It was a tiny sterling Scientology symbol on a chain, one she'd been admiring for months. "Thank you so much! And you totally fooled me!" She gave me a kiss, and fastened it round her neck.

We had Christmas dinner at Threadgill's, famous for its Texas, southern-style cooking. Big helpings of black eyed peas, macaroni and cheese and little squares of sweet corn bread finished off with sugary pumpkin pie for dessert. "Mmm, this is so good."

Cedar leaned back in her chair, loudly smacking her lips and then looked around, embarrassed.

We stayed in Austin one more day, visiting a dozen more second-hand shops, which really are one-of-a-kind. Ed and I piled mountains of clothes into plastic bags, stuffing them into all the remaining cracks and corners of the van.

On our way home we stopped in New Orleans. "I love it here," Cedar reminded me as we walked down Royal Street, rubbernecking in the European antique shops.

Ed was in The Louisiana Music Factory, the premier blues music record store on Decatur Street. Musicians sometimes performed on a tiny stage right in the middle of the store, but Ed was there to sift through used CDs. We decided to meet in an hour and drive a little further, where the motels were cheaper.

After a Waffle House breakfast the next morning we headed home. It was a long drive, through three more states. By the time it turned dark, Cedar was sitting in the front seat co-piloting with an open map spread out on her lap. I lay on the bed in the back of the van, drifting in and out of sleep all the way down Highway 19 toward home, listening to Ed and Cedar laughing softly and talking over the sound of the engine.

50

THE FLORIDA HOUSE

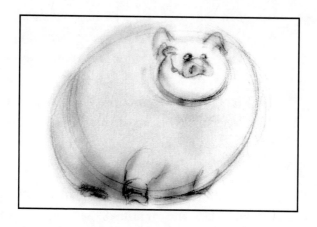

Ed and I had a new friend named Lee, a thin, dapper man with silver hair and a surprisingly wicked sense of humor. He and his pragmatic wife Delon were in their late forties, like us. They were Bob and Nancy's friends, introduced to us at Nancy's last Thanksgiving party. "You should buy a house in Clearwater," Delon told us when we complained about running our business from a two-bedroom apartment. The two of them remodeled houses for a living, buying and selling fixer-uppers. They knew everything going on in the real estate market locally. But I wasn't enthusiastic.

"We just don't have the money right now," I reminded Ed.

He pointed out that our rent money was going down a bottomless hole, but I said "We can't buy a house for seven hundred dollars a month," which was where our rent had settled after two years.

Lee introduced Ed to a real estate maestro named Michel, who had agreed to help. He was a portly Canadian gentleman with curling grey hair worn a little long and combed neatly back. For weeks all I knew of him was that smooth and romantic French accented voice over the phone, because he picked Ed up in his luxury Mercedes every afternoon to tour the latest possibilities on the multiple listing service. I did not go with them.

One late afternoon in June, Ed bounded up the stairs to our apartment. "I found a house that comes with a farm animal!"

"What?!" I was mixing clay and making little horse-head earrings, but Ed said Michel was waiting for us and we had to go right now.

"Can Cedar come?"

"Of course! But we need to hurry." Cedar was working on her latest project, a children's book she was writing and illustrating. It was about a fat cat that ate asparagus and the dignified servant who carried him around on a pillow. It was based on Molly, who used to gobble asparagus and then throw up.

"Oh, okay," she said, unenthused, after I knocked on her door to explain. She hated being interrupted.

302

Ed introduced us to Michel, then Cedar and I sank into the leather back seat. "What kind of farm animal?" I asked.

Michel laughed and Ed looked at me in his masculine version of coyness; raised eyebrows and a tight-lipped smile. "You'll see."

We pulled up to a house painted hospital green. It was set back from the street on an overgrown lawn with a straggly red climbing rose listing sadly off a front porch pillar. I wanted to see the animal first thing, so Ed led Cedar and me around to the back yard. There was a small area with a chain link fence on the west side. Before I could see what was in it, I heard the snorting.

"It's a pig!" Cedar laughed.

Michel had joined us. "Her name is Audrey. She's a pot-bellied pig and she belonged to the little boy who lived here with his dad." It was a sad story. The child's father died suddenly of a complication after surgery and the house was being sold by his brothers.

"If you decide to take it, the seller will find a new home for the pig. That is, if you don't want to keep her." Audrey gazed up at us with red rheumy eyes, her wide black girth filling half the pen. I'd always thought pot-bellied pigs were small and cute.

"No, I don't think we'd keep her," I replied evenly and Cedar looked relieved.

We walked across an expanse of green cement, a pathway to the door of the Florida room. Inside we faced the backyard through a wall of windows. This entire room was painted salmon pink in two shades—even the floor tiles hinted at it. *A person had actually chosen those colors,* I thought wonderingly.

This view of the backyard, deep into the rainy season was brilliant green and overgrown. Butterflies danced around a purple blooming hedge that grew under gnarled oak branches. "I don't see any fruit trees," I mentioned to Michel.

"No, you'll have to plant your own," he answered jovially, as if the deed were signed.

Our tour took us up two steps from the Florida room into a small kitchen painted the same dark salmon except for one wall someone had covered in wallpaper that looked like burlap. All the cabinets had a wood grain look, dirty white above countertops with 'seventies era sparkles and swirls.

The living room fireplace was an organically pleasing puzzle of large shale pieces in grays and browns, but the mantel was constructed of rough planks with an oak veneer glued over it. Cedar lifted the veneer up on the corner by the wall. I laughed, but Ed said, "Hey you guys, leave that alone!"

I was leaning against the long wall separating the living room from the Florida room when it buckled inward. "What the..." It was just paneling, painted the same dirty yellow as the other walls, seemingly free standing.

"Oh, that can be replaced with dry wall." Michel pointed out airily. "You have to imagine the inside with a fresh coat of paint," he went on. "It's a very well made house. The original owner built it in 1948." That explained the lack of cabinets in the kitchen, I thought to myself.

But it also explained the oak floors and thick wooden molding in the living room and bedrooms. There were occasional deco touches, a high glass lamp in one of the hallways and decorative covers for the fuse boxes. Most of the original 1940s beauty had been *modernized* by later owners and tenants, but it was a house with good bones.

It was also a project—almost every room, including both baths, needed wallpaper stripping, odd addition removals, (like the corner TV stand built into one bedroom) refinishing of the oak floors and, of course, the new wall in the living room. The pink tiles would have to go—they were cracked in the kitchen anyway. Painting was the least of it. But the price was unbelievable in the current market.

We talked it over back at the apartment. "I'm afraid if we take it we won't really fix it up. We have these great intentions but this house really is a project." I was thinking about our home in California; the second bathroom we never put in, the new carpeting never laid.

"No, we will fix this one up," Ed assured me, his eyes steady.

It closed when we were out of state, so we bought it long distance, signing dozens of papers in a title company office in California. We had just finished an art show in San Jose and drove up to Rough and Ready to check on our house there and find a new tenant, someone whose rent we hoped would actually cover our mortgage.

On the flight home we talked about the future. Ed said "We have two houses now, and something to leave the kids." He took my hand and I leaned back, dreaming of a future with Cedar in it.

51

COLORS

Cedar and I checked out dozens of library books on decorating. "Look, here's one that tells you how to turn thrift store junk into beautiful hand-painted furniture!" We spent hours flipping through pages, sent off on flights of creative fancy. This had nothing to do with stripping wallpaper and painting.

It took a week to remove it all, an infestation that spread into the hallway by the kitchen, across the house to one of the bedroom walls on the other side and into both bathrooms. Maybe the perpetrator had several free rolls, or maybe they actually liked it. But I found this hard to believe. Ed did most of this work, sponging offending walls to sloppy damp then sliding a paint scraper across the dissolving burlappy mess.

Cedar and I attended a Home Depot demonstration, watching a sturdy middle-aged lady sponge and drag rags of color over drywall for interesting effects. In the end we painted all the rooms off-white, including the once dark salmon kitchen. That was a miracle of latex paint chemistry, I thought, as the dreaded color disappeared forever beneath my roller.

Cedar chose pale lavender for her own room, just the other side of white. It was more of a stain than a color. She had a vision for her room and afterwards painted the old wooden bed she'd had since she was five years old a deep burgundy, with sloppy streaks across the headboard and legs. It would be an expanse of drama against her delicate wall canvas.

Cedar wore baggy white trousers and an old sleeveless t-shirt while she worked, sloshing paint buckets across the floor and whistling. "Cedar! Watch the drips!" The floors were refinished now, the oak boards restored to a golden shine. Paint spots wiped up easily and I followed her across the room with a damp rag.

We moved in before all the painting was finished. One of Cedar's dance partners was finagled into helping us with the heavy stuff. It was poor Brian, of course. I think he loved Cedar because whatever she asked him to do he would, even giving up a Saturday boating on the bay for sore muscles and a constant sheen of sweat. I think his pay was pizza and a fifty dollar bill… and Cedar's company, of course.

Everything had been carted into appropriate rooms, boxes and furniture stacked into an organized jumble. At eight thirty, Cedar flopped onto the loveseat, long lean arms and legs sprawled across its width. "I'm exhausted!" Brian had gone and the only thing left to do that night was put sheets on the mattresses and sleep. I pried Cedar into bed then fell onto my own mattress, where Ed, oblivious to the pandemonium, was already snoring.

ƒEPTEMBEꞦ 11

E d and I set up our studio in the Florida room where we could watch lizards scurry across the outside windowsill and butterflies drift through the flowering bushes. Since we had no computers yet, my drafting table was covered with tools and globs of colored clay in varying degrees of transformation.

On September 11, Ed was working on our yearly calendar. He slit open a fat envelope. "Well, we're accepted into a great show in Pittsburgh, but we're in a Florida show the same weekend."

I groaned. "Wouldn't you know it?"

Cedar sat at a folding table between our two workspaces, addressing bubble envelopes and stuffing them with colorful jewelry orders displayed on aqua colored cards. "This person has a funny name—Tristan Oglethorpe!" Cedar laughed. "Maybe I can use it in my next screenplay."

"I'm sure he'd be honored," I said.

After lunch Ed called our old mortgage broker in California, asking Jess if he knew anyone to manage our Rough and Ready property. Our new tenants paid their rent for the first two months, long enough for Ed and me to congratulate ourselves on having a little financial wisdom after all. But on the second day of September the wife called to engage our sympathy with her struggles to keep up. "My husband was accused of molesting our daughter, then he skipped bail and we have no idea where he is." This story made my skin crawl and now forced us to find a new tenant long distance.

"What? Oh No!" It was unusual for Ed's equilibrium to be rattled. Had they burned our house down too?

"No, we haven't had the radio on all day, and you're the first person we've talked to outside the house. We'll turn it on now. Thanks for letting us know." He hung up.

I looked at Ed. "What's going on?"

He sat in the chair silently, still absorbing whatever Jess had said. Then, "Two planes hit the World Trade Center in New York and both buildings were destroyed."

We turned on the radio at two o' clock that afternoon, possibly the last people in the country to hear about the September 11 attacks. Was this the beginning of some end? Even the newscasters sounded worried. We had no television, so didn't see the planes crashing into the buildings until much later, or the famous clip of George Bush talking to school children when the fatal words were whispered in his ear.

When I called my brother's house in Brooklyn that evening, his wife answered. "Are you guys okay?" I asked Lynne.

"Yes, we're fine, except both Alex and I had to walk home from work today."

"Isn't that an impossible distance?"

"Yes, it was miles. But at least we got home safely."

"What's it like there now?"

"The sky is filled with debris; papers have been floating all the way to our neighborhood from Lower Manhattan."

We kept the radio on for days, listening to newscasters, bereaved survivors, policemen and conspiracy theorists. It was the only news, and every station carried miniscule updates without pause. Like everyone else in the country, we were waiting for another attack, as if three thousand dead were not bad enough.

I was still painting walls. I remember rolling white over the dirty yellow living room while desperate relatives pleaded for news of loved ones on the radio. I'd cry when an especially poignant act of heroism was retold or a distressed mother begged the audience for information to help her find a missing daughter, wiping my eyes with my sleeve, the roller held carefully at arm's length.

This shadow of death and uncertainty reminded me of the cold war, when we were told that on any day, nukes might fall and climbing under our school desks would be a drill no longer. Thousands of people I'd never know were now gone, and I wondered how it must have been for them. I pictured a well dressed secretary sipping her Starbucks coffee and typing a memo just before being plunged into fiery chaos.

It seemed strange that the mundane parts of life continued, but of course they had to.

Cedar was taking a class at our church during the day and Ed filled out applications for upcoming 2002 art shows. Lately, we had added Veterinary Conferences to our schedule of shows. Exhibiting my animal-themed jewelry at an event where everybody's profession was taking care of pets seemed like a good idea, and my booth in these conference halls was usually crowded.

Other changes were afoot. I'd grown tired of making everything by hand, and recently discovered that my work could be cast in sterling silver.

"Mommy, that's so great!" Cedar hated me spending all my time re-making the same designs, irritated by boredom and sore wrists. She wanted me to start singing again. I had had a mini-renaissance after Terry's death and was recording some of my own songs on the little tape machine Ed had given me for my last birthday.

"Well, we'll see how it goes. I don't even know for sure that anyone will buy this new stuff."

"Of course they will!" She'd watched my first models emerge—the stately Egyptian cat pin, the African Grey pendant with intricately carved wings, my first Labrador retriever earrings. "They're beautiful, Mom." She hugged me as I sat at my drafting table putting some finishing touches on the cat.

53

OCTOBER

Cedar said to me once, "I hate the fact that I was born in October. Every store is decorated with Halloween stuff and *that's* what everybody associates with this month."

"There's not too much I can do about it now," I laughed. Cedar had spent most of her life in year-round warmth, so autumn leaves and changing seasons meant little to her.

On her last birthday, October 4, 2001 we gave Cedar two tickets to see Chuck Berry and Little Richard. They would be playing at Ruth Eckerd Hall on October 25, nine days after we would have left for two art shows in the northeast.

"Where do you want to eat for your birthday dinner?" I was home with her on the fourth, but Ed was already exhibiting at an art show in Maryland.

She picked the local Mexican place on Drew Street. Cedar loved bean and cheese burritos and they served gigantic ones there. When we walked into the restaurant, the waiter looked up and blushed.

"He likes you!" I whispered to Cedar after he seated her.

"I know, it's so cute," Cedar said to me quietly.

Over dinner we talked about our trip to California, planned for the end of November. Cedar hadn't seen her brother in five years and we were going to have a Thanksgiving dinner reunion right before the Veterinary conference Ed and I had scheduled in San Diego.

David had missed Cedar's growth into womanhood, and I missed seeing them together. They were constantly trying to out-tease and out-joke each other; at least that's how it had been five years before. The memory made me smile and helped pass my thoughts quickly over the rest of October, which I dreaded.

The president sent troops to Afghanistan on October 7, the same day I was to fly to Portland, Oregon for a show.

Cedar was driving me to the airport. We were crossing the causeway early in the morning so I could catch my plane from Tampa International. "Cedar, I forgot my jewelry!"

"Oh Mom, how could you do that?" We were halfway to the airport.

"I think I left it in the driveway when we were loading my suitcase." We had to go back; I could still barely catch my plane if we hurried. We sped down Gulf to Bay Boulevard, willing lights to turn green and cars to let us pass. We made it home in twenty minutes.

The carry-on with all my jewelry in it sat benignly in the middle of the driveway.

Our local junkman, the old man with the giant tricycle who looked through everyone's trash hadn't been by yet. I sighed, threw open the car door and tossed it in. I was jittery anyway, afraid my plane would blow up halfway across the country. "Cedar, if anything happens to me, remember how much I love you."

"What? Mom, don't say things like that!" She was appalled.

"I'm sorry. I just wish I didn't have to leave you now." I arrived in Portland without incident, of course.

The show was busy. It was a convention for competing women's singing groups, and attendees came from all over the world. One of my first customers, a woman from New York, told me her best friend had lost a son in the World Trade Center attacks. "He was their only son and now their lives are over."

"I'm so sorry," I said, reaching for her hand.

The show went surprisingly well, and on the flight back to Tampa I was comforted that at least one October dread had passed.

Ed and I were packed and ready to leave on October 16, but Cedar was upset about something and I hated to go. "Mom, I had a *terrible* dream."

"What was it?" I asked cautiously. Cedar had her psychic moments and the tone of her voice made me feel cold.

"I can't tell you," she said miserably.

"Oh, Baby, I'm sure everything will be okay." Then Cedar hugged me, holding me in an embrace that lasted several minutes, a hug I have never forgotten and can still feel. I know exactly where we stood, can hear Ed outside the studio door reminding me to hurry, the van starting up, a single mocking bird singing an exuberant medley, the pressure and warmth of her body against mine.

When she let me go her face was calm. "You guys better go."

I kissed her. "I'll call you tonight."

When we got to our motel around seven, I called and she sounded better, with a little bounce in her voice. "I'm going dancing tonight, so I'm in a really good mood." I'd just gotten into bed, sinking into sweet smelling sheets, pointing my toes and stretching after an eight-hour drive.

"I'm so glad. Just have fun and don't worry about anything. This time will go fast and we'll be back soon. I love you, Baby."

"I love you, too."

Our first stop was in Pennsylvania, the reason we had left a few days early. I was needed for an in-person appearance to jury for some prestigious show. "Thank you but your work isn't what we are looking for at this time." I fumed, thinking of Cedar and wasted days apart.

After that Ed and I were doing two separate shows, but we had a few days before either of them started. We spent them in New York, and because 9-11 was just behind us, we made a pilgrimage to the sight of the disaster.

It was when the steel skeletons still stood and caravans of trucks worked constantly hauling out the buildings' remains. The air was acrid with chemicals and decomposition. Signs with messages to loved ones and flowers edged the sidewalk in front of a church and the New Yorkers we passed were uncharacteristically quiet.

That night we spent at Alex and Lynne's house in Brooklyn. Several of their neighbors had been lost in the tragedy, firefighters and policemen. The houses on his street, skinny side-by-side brownstones and Victorians all had American flags angled from stands attached to their front porches. The air was fall crisp and Alex's front yard maple had turned to gold.

I called Cedar that night. She was buzzing with excitement over a new project. "Mom, I'm drawing cartoons—I can't wait for you to see them!"

"It won't be too long now. We'll be home in less than a week!" I didn't mention our journey to Lower Manhattan but described how Alex had completely remodeled his kitchen with the help of a few friends, then described the fluorescent orange and red of a spectacular northeast autumn.

"I'm so glad you're getting to spend some time with Alex and Lynne."

"I am too. Hold on while I get Dad. I love you, Baby."

"I love you, too."

I passed the phone to Ed and joined Alex and his young son Kirby who were tossing a football in their narrow back yard. Alex is just about my height, maybe an inch taller—5 feet 7 or so. Alex had a goatee that fall, his hair a little on the long side, just over his collar. He was still wearing his work khakis covered with about fifty different colors of paint. He looked up at me with intense hazel eyes. "Everything okay?"

"Oh, sure. Cedar's been busy, which is always a good thing." Alex found my daughter an enigma. She had come for a visit a few years earlier amidst a time of teen angst, and truthfully had upset her uncle by arguing over the merits of a Broadway show he had taken her to.

Alex was working as an artist on Broadway sets at the time, a good gig—union. He was up early the next morning, drinking coffee and rattling the paper in the kitchen, right next to the living room where we slept on a pull-out couch. I got up and joined him. "Hi, Poopface." This was the Hutton sibling greeting that made all of our children giggle.

"Are you and Ed taking off this morning?"

"Yep. He goes to New Jersey and I drive to Rhode Island."

He looked at me sympathetically. "But you'll have fun staying with Holly." Our sister lived in East Greenwich, just about an hour from the show I'd be doing in Boston.

"Okay, I've got to go." His ride was honking her car horn and Alex gave me a quick hug on his way out.

Lynne and Kirby came downstairs after we had packed and were ready to leave. "I hope you both have good shows," she said in her ghost of a soft southern accent. Lynne is a tall woman, with a sweet sounding, easy laugh and a thick mop of curly dark hair worn short.

Kirby, now eight years old but still unembarrassed by hugs, put his arms around my waist while I tousled his hair. "Goodbye, Sweetie. Take care of your parents." Ed shook his hand with mock formality.

I drove Ed to his show in New Jersey and then spent a half hour with him writing maps in big letters that I could read easily while driving to Holly's. I was morose.

"I don't want to leave you."

"You'll have fun at Holly's. And don't forget, Maggie's helping you set up the show tomorrow." Maggie was Holly's daughter, just a year younger than Cedar. My earliest memories of the two of them were at Holly's old home outside Chicago, where we visited her family back in the early 1980s. I have a photo of Holly and me holding our little girls up to nurse, but it was posed since Maggie was already weaned by then. By the second grade Cedar and Maggie were pen-pals, writing letters back in forth in misspelled pencil scrawls. They shared flower-girl duties at Alex's wedding and teenaged secrets during family reunions. Later I found out that Maggie had known about Cedar losing her virginity before I did.

"You're right. I know I'm being silly." We kissed goodbye.

Five hours later I pulled up to Holly's house, parking on the street instead of her steep driveway that always feels a little uncertain in a heavy van. Chuck, her husband and my friend from long ago, opened the door and we hugged. "How was your trip?" Chuck is my age, a few years younger than my sister. He's a short man, but sturdily built with a deep and certain voice. This is perfect for the political aspirations he's had, and for the good things he promotes on radio and TV for his community. Many years earlier we'd met as fellow actors in a play back in Ohio. Despite my mother's suspicions, our friendship was never anything but platonic.

"Oh, it was okay. Where's Holly?"

"She had a Pilates class after work. She said she'll be home about eight."

I called our house, hoping to catch Cedar before she went somewhere for the night. At that time we had one of those answering machines that beeps for every call that's been recorded. I counted seventeen, an awful lot of unanswered messages.

Cedar must have been out all day. Maybe she'd gone to her Halloween party right from class.

I helped Chuck pass out candy to trick-or-treaters. When Holly got home Chuck went to bed and Holly and I gossiped about our children. She was looking marvelous, as usual. In shape, still attractive, temporarily makeup free. Strangers tell us we look alike, but when we were teenagers I felt ugly next to her slim good looks and delicate features.

It's funny because when I look at those old photos I wonder what I worried about. We didn't look the same back then, but I did have my own appeal.

"Maggie is going to join the Air Force!" Holly told me, wonderingly. She already had one child in the Air Force, Chip, who was stationed in Texas. Her other son, Taylor, was still in college studying to be a teacher.

"Wow, that's sure a change." The last I knew Maggie was headed for college in Ohio, a party school that Holly wasn't so thrilled with.

"Where *is* Maggie?"

"She's out with her friends but she said 'Tell Crazy Aunt Merry that I definitely want to help her set up the show.'"

"Do you suppose she knows what she's in for?" I asked Holly.

I fell asleep easily in our grandmother's old spindle bed, placed in the computer room upstairs.

I woke up about eight the next morning, later than I should have. I could hear voices downstairs, Holly's and a man's. That seemed strange. I thought Chuck had left for work much earlier. I got up and showered.

I walked downstairs, turned the corner to the kitchen and found Ed sitting with Holly at the table. I was so happy to see him that the oddness of it all wasn't the first thing to hit me. "Hi baby! Was your show canceled? Will you do the one in Boston with me?" I was full of good cheer at this development.

Holly had a funny look on her face and Ed wasn't frowning but not smiling either.

"Was there another terrorist attack?" My heart beat faster.

I looked at Holly. "No…"

Ed said "Merry, we should go outside." He was calm, purposeful, serious.

"Is it Cedar? Has something happened to her?" Ed was edging me towards the front door. "What's going on?" He silently guided me out the door, onto the side yard, onto the damp emerald grass with tall trees behind us and the neighbor's golden retrievers barking at us through the fence.

Ed embraced me, his leather jacket cool under my hands. It made a creaking noise as he held me tighter. "What's happened to Cedar? Is she in the hospital? Tell me!" In the same terrified instant I was trying to both know and not know the truth.

"Merry, she's gone."

"No, no, no, no, no!"

"Mandy and Laura called me in my hotel last night. She died the night before, about an hour after we talked to her. She was on the phone with Brian and when she stopped talking and wouldn't answer him, he called the police." I was sobbing, holding Ed, straining against this nightmare under a too brilliant sky, trying not to collapse.

"Ed, we have to go back, right now. She needs us there." I pictured our poor lost soul alone in the house and it was more than I could bear. "We have to fly home today," I sobbed.

"We'll see. I think it would be good to drive, get some space, just the two of us."

We walked slowly back to the house, to make arrangements, to say goodbye.

Holly promised to call our siblings and our mom, while Maggie and I cried and hugged. I told her, "It helps to hold a pretty young girl."

Maggie apologized, "I'm sorry I'm not as skinny as Cedar." An incongruous burst of laughter from both of us, quickly drowned.

On the trip home I sobbed for hours without a break. It made me thirsty, all that violent bawling. "I would trade any body part of mine to have her back," I told Ed. "I'd give up my eyes, my hearing, I wouldn't care."

"I know, Baby," Ed said quietly.

It seemed like Cedar was nearby, and when it turned dark I imagined her leading us gracefully and quietly home to Clearwater.

"I think she's somewhere out there dancing," Ed told me quietly. He put on a Jerry Lee Lewis tape.

54

THE DREAM

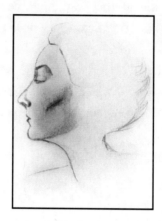

We got back home at midnight, two days later. The front windows had plywood over them where the police had broken in so the paramedics could get to Cedar. Glass was scattered across the living room floor, and I got out the broom to sweep it up.

The dishes from her last meal filled the sink. She'd had noodles and nutritional yeast, still her favorite and one she could make easily herself. "Oh Ed, I can't stand it!"

"Come here. You don't have to do this now. Let's go to bed."

I lay awake, staring into space, trying to see where she'd gone.

The next morning, neighbors we barely knew came by with sad eyes to ask if there was anything they could do. A woman down the street brought brownies and I still don't know who she was because Ed had taken them from her at the door while I sat at the kitchen table, lost in sorrow. Hank, an African-American ex-con who lived in the yellow house directly across the street, hugged me gently and said he'd pray for our family. He was the one who had nailed up the plywood. Lottie, a white haired Octogenarian from three houses down shook her head sadly and told me she felt cheated that now she'd never get to know Cedar beyond their friendly morning waves.

Ed called the Neptune Society, to ask about cremation. In the middle of a sentence he broke into sobs and I heard him apologizing to the woman on the other end. "What a job to have," I thought.

On our first night driving home from Rhode Island we had called David. He had been quiet on the other end; holding his grief so it wouldn't spill over the line. It was excruciating to give him this news thousands of miles away from our physical comfort, but there was no other way. We made arrangements for him to fly to Tampa on November 5.

We drove to the airport to pick him up and parked outside Continental's baggage claim. "See you in a minute." I kissed Ed and took the escalator to where the debarking passengers got off the tram.

I spotted him, tall and muscled, wearing his old green raincoat and a pair of leather work boots, just leaving the tram. "David!" He strode towards me, smiling down as we hugged.

"Hi Mom," he put his arm around my shoulders as we headed towards the escalator and baggage claim. A tired brown suitcase was expelled from the luggage machine and rotated towards us. David grabbed it easily and we went outside. Ed was leaning against the Volvo with his arms crossed. The two men embraced and we headed home.

Later that afternoon, David held my hand without embarrassment, walking with me down the bike trail across the street from our house, pointing out trees and signs. It helped, focusing outward.

Six days after Cedar died, Ed and David went to the funeral home to arrange the cremation. I stayed home, put Beethoven's 9th on the CD player and turned it up loud. I pretended to be that great musician, wildly conducting the glorious tapestry of sound he'd created completely from memory.

I wanted her back. I knew it made me sound crazy, but that's what I told people—my friends who wanted to help and asked me what I needed. "I need her to come back to me," I said simply. I felt like all her clothes and everything she used should be kept in readiness.

I imagined waking up from the worst nightmare I'd ever had, and there she would be, laughing at me for being such a worry wart, or mad at me that I'd even *have* a dream where she could die.

I washed the clothes she had worn that last week, neatly folded them and made little stacks before putting them in her drawers. I didn't change her sheets or pillowcase though. I couldn't bear to lose her scent completely.

The black notebook with the cartoons she had told me about the last time we talked was sitting on a table in the studio. They were full of observations on her friends, funny caricatures of herself and the rockabilly dancers she'd spent so much time with. On one page she had drawn her ideal man, with notes on "What a Boyfriend Ought to be"— polite, a non-drinker, non-smoker, non-drug taker, very ethical, stylish, a good dancer.

At night, I lay on her bed with my eyes shut, willing her to come to me. Cedar was near. I felt her, helpless in another dimension but just out of my reach. I wept.

ſong for Cedar

I wished Ed, David and I could live in a cocoon during that week. I didn't want to see anyone but Cedar's closest friends, who came by with hot meals to commiserate.

But our families would start arriving for the memorial service by the next day. "How are we going to entertain them?" I looked at Ed miserably.

"You don't entertain anyone. That's hardly the point."

My mom, Jeff and Reda arrived on the morning of November 8, two days before the service. I felt a strange embarrassment around them, like I'd carelessly misplaced my daughter's life.

I brushed off their sympathy and took them on a bright-voiced tour of our house. "We've done a lot to the house since we bought it, but there's a lot more fixing up..." I breezed through the half-done kitchen into the living room.

"I don't care about the damn house," Mom announced after I'd pointed out the interesting pattern of the slate fireplace. She burst into tears.

Kate, now 87, was hurt that I had never told her about Cedar's heart condition. I was honest. "Mom, I didn't think you would outlive Cedar. What would be the purpose of upsetting you?"

Holly and Maggie arrived that afternoon in a sporty red rental car with Alex in the back seat. Their flights from New York and Rhode Island had magically coordinated.

Alex drove with me to Wal-Mart to purchase frames for two of Cedar's drawings we planned to display at her memorial service. On the way back, I wept.

"Do you want me to drive?" he asked, alarmed.

"No, I'm sorry." I pulled over. The tears were unpredictable. Once I'd sobbed uncontrollably in the middle of the pasta aisle at Publix. Annie's macaroni and cheese had been Cedar's favorite lunch.

That afternoon I took a walk with Holly and Maggie. They'd been with us when the nightmare unfolded and their good-humored mutual haranguing cheered me a little. "When do you leave for boot camp?" I asked Maggie.

"Next week."

"She's really looking forward to camping outside with the lizards and bugs." Holly looked at Maggie sidelong, grinning. We'd had a long-standing joke that our daughters weren't "nature girls" like us. I showed Maggie how to shoo lizards away by bending over and clapping my hands, chasing a terrified anole. We laughed.

Holly and Maggie cooked dinner that night—spaghetti served on wooden boards and metal sawhorses set up in the studio to accommodate everyone. I had no tablecloths to fit them so we ate on sheets, joking about the ambience.

"Let Maggie and me wash the dishes." Holly was stern, barring my way to the sink.

"I have to do something," I told her. There was an ancient normality to doing the dishes with my sister, a lull to some past before adulthood, and children.

"Does Scientology have grief counseling?" Holly was looking at me, concerned.

"We don't call it that, but yes, I'll definitely get some Scientology counseling. All of us will."

"I'm glad."

The next day, Jeff and David put a door in our studio to hide the air conditioning unit. "This is how I deal with grief," Jeff told me. "I build things." He talked to me alone once, in the threshold of the side garage door. Jeff is a large man, blond with well muscled arms and broad shoulders. He looked down at me thoughtfully and said "You are so lucky to have had her. Reda and I weren't able to have kids. Be grateful you had her in your life for twenty years."

"I am." I smiled at him.

On Friday, tiny, dark-eyed Susan and now white-bearded Larry arrived from New York with their two teenagers. "Is there anything we can do?" Susan looked up at me sympathetically.

"No, you guys should get some rest. I think there's an indoor pool at the hotel." I looked at Jessie and Rebecca. "Did you kids bring bathing suits?"

Our niece Rebecca stood quietly, her soft features dusted with grief for her cousin. A year earlier she'd come to spend a week with us, dancing at night with Cedar and her friends, watching videos until midnight in our apartment. She stayed in Cedar's room, the two of them whispering and talking until two in the morning. One late afternoon we baked chocolate chip cookies together and drove to the beach at sunset, floating and laughing in green lukewarm water, surrounded by sticky seaweed. "Yes, we did bring them, but I'd rather just hang out," she answered with a faint smile.

Jessie stood next to his dad, almost Larry's height now, his lanky frame somewhere between boy and manhood. His

curly auburn hair was short, tight against his scalp. "How
are you doing, Jessie?" I put my arm around his thin waist.

"Okay, I guess," he smiled crookedly.

That night Mom decided we needed to get out of the
house and took all of us to the local Thai restaurant to dine on
her favorite cuisine. Jeff made a toast to Cedar, comparing
her meteoric life to the blinding burst of a supernova. Jeff is
an amateur astronomer, and when Cedar spent a weekend
with him eleven months earlier, he had shown her the Orion
Nebula through the telescope he'd built.

The following morning, Peter and Sue arrived from
San Francisco, exhausted from the red eye. We had only
two hours until the memorial service. I sat with Sue on
Cedar's bed. "I'm so sorry you never met her. She
would've loved having you in the family." She sat quietly,
her slim frame poised delicately, holding a photograph of
Cedar taken at a costume party two days before her death.

Two days earlier we had called Peter at home in
California to see if he would take us on their boat *The
Seabird* to scatter Cedar's ashes in late November. "Of
course," he said, unhesitating. Peter worked as a ferry
captain operating in the San Francisco Bay. He and Sue
lived on *The Seabird*, their renovated trawler with three
miniature bedrooms, beautifully finished in polished wood
paneling, now anchored at a marina in San Rafael.

Cedar's memorial service was on a Saturday, in a
privately owned hall in downtown Clearwater. "What

was Cedar's favorite flower?" Reda asked me several days earlier.

"I gave her white carnations after every performance. I know she loved those."

Reda ordered hundreds of them, filling the room with their fragrance and Hollywood-in-the-'30s opulence, so perfect.

"I'm so glad Cedar came to spend time with us last February," Reda told me softly, her brown eyes tearing up. Ed and I had taken Cedar with us to Ohio for a Veterinary conference in Columbus and ended up leaving her with my family in nearby Alexandria, Kentucky while we did the show. Jeff and Reda spent two days showing her the deco wonders of Old Cincinnati.

"She told me she had the best time with you and Jeff, and was so grateful she got to know you better," I said. Reda smiled sadly.

The large room was filling up. Cedar's family and friends, people who had worked with her on plays, fellow Scientology students, even her dentist, Dr. Charlie. A contingent of her rockabilly crowd sat in the back, looking at the floor. "I'm so glad you came." I gave each of them a hug.

"We feel a little out of place," Mike said, looking at his lineup of tattooed and pompadoured friends.

"It's perfectly fine," I told him.

Our friend Bob delivered the service, wearing his ministerial collar and reading from a service written by L. Ron Hubbard over thirty five years earlier. The words were beautiful, but I couldn't connect them with my daughter's death. Toward the end, when the congregation says goodbye to the departed, I whispered, "Don't leave yet."

I stood up with my dulcimer and turned to play an Appalachian ballad about a lost love, with the words changed only slightly to fit. "Oh Fare-thee-well my own dear child…" Cedar had loved my voice, and singing for her now, I felt joyful and free, surprising myself.

My sister read a biblical passage from Ecclesiastes, "To everything there is a season, and a time to every purpose under the heaven: A time to be born, and a time to die; a time to plant, and a time to pluck up that which is planted…" Holly was doing well until she saw Alex crying, then she stumbled her way through the rest, sobbing in commiseration.

Ed stood to talk, his body trembling. "Cedar had the best sense of humor. She loved to hear about her Jewish heritage, and recently…" he paused, catching his train of thought and suppressing a gulp of sorrow, "I read this joke to her from *The Joys of Yiddish* …" Ed read it again with a European Jewish accent, and we all laughed at the joke, which was about a psychiatrist. I pictured Cedar at the breakfast table, throwing back her head and guffawing.

One of her dance partners walked to the front to speak. He stared nervously towards the back of the hall from the podium. "Cedar was generous with everyone. I realize I don't look like most people, but Cedar didn't mind. She cared about all her friends equally and I'll always love her for that…" He wiped away a tear. "I never got to tell her how much she meant to me, but from now on, all the people I love will know how I feel."

We'd planned a rockabilly dance at the end, something I was positive Cedar wanted at her service. But when David put on *Great Balls of Fire* her friends looked stunned. *How could we possibly dance at a time like this?* was the clear message on their faces.

"Cedar loved dancing with you," I reminded them. "It'd make her happy if you could do this for her."

They did, slowly and hesitatingly at first, trying to be respectful. "Come on, dance!" I could hear Cedar shouting, and they sped up, twirling and jiving all across the empty space at the back of the hall, as though they were back at the Italian Club in Ybor City.

The service was over. We filled up our car with carnations and packed up the leftover food to feed our families for another half day.

The next morning Mom ate breakfast with us. "Will you be all right? I don't know what I would have done if one of you all had died." She was packed and waiting for Ed to drive the three of them to the airport.

Jeff and Reda hugged me, telling me to call if I needed something, anything from them.

"Thanks," I smiled.

Holly and Maggie were already gone, and Susan and her family would be leaving within the hour.

"Alex, when do you go?" I asked him. I'd lost track of everybody's departure schedule.

"Susan and Larry will take me to the airport on their way out of town," he said.

That was it. David was leaving in another two days, back to L.A. In less than two weeks we'd pick him up there after our show in San Diego and the three of us would drive to San Francisco to scatter Cedar's ashes. "I wish you weren't leaving," I said to him wistfully that evening.

He smiled at me. "I'll be seeing you and Dad again soon."

After David had gone to bed, Ed and I sat at the kitchen table. "I'm not ready to stop being a parent," I told him. We looked at each other miserably.

56

Farewell, Dear Child

On November 21, we set sail on *The Sea Bird*. Rick and Sue sat quietly with us on the deck. Cedar's ashes were in a beautiful box David had built to contain them, brought with us on the plane from Clearwater.

Peter piloted us toward the Golden Gate Bridge, and when the right spot was reached, Ed, David and I read this poem by Arthur O'Shaughnessy, each of us throwing one verse to the wind, straining against the sounds of motor and wake.

"We are the music makers,
And we are the dreamers of dreams,
Wandering by lone sea breakers,
And sitting by desolate streams.
World-losers and world-forsakers,
On whom the pale moon gleams:
Yet we are the movers and shakers
Of the world forever it seems

"With wonderful deathless ditties
We build up the world's great cities,
We fashion an empire's glory:
One man with a dream at pleasure,
Shall go forth and conquer a crown;
And three with a new song's measure
Can trample an empire down.

"We, in the ages lying,
In the buried past of the earth,
Built Nineveh with our sighing,
And Babel itself with our mirth;
And o'erthrew them with prophesying
To the old of the new world's worth;
For each age is a dream that is dying,
Or one that is coming to birth..."

Now Peter stopped the boat and joined us on the deck. We opened the box and each of us took a handful of soft grey ash, tossing it into the sea along with some autumn chrysanthemums. An irregular trail of blooms and ash followed in the wake of the drifting boat. When a breeze picked up some ash and blew it back towards us, I thought I could hear her laughing. "Just like a Laurel and Hardy bit," Ed said softly, so only David and I could hear.

57

EPILOGUE

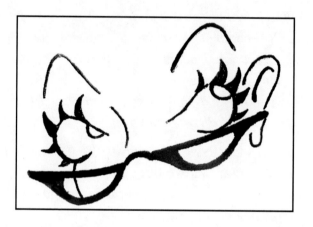

Eight years have passed since Cedar died. The first few months were nearly impossible. I couldn't walk into her bedroom without a shiver of unreality and grief. I spent hours looking at her drawings and re-reading her plays and stories. I was obsessed by the idea of finding something I'd missed, a note or drawing that would seem like a fresh communication from her.

I discovered a diary recording her first tender, awkward moments with the opposite sex, a piece of paper with directions to a dance club, and, most poignant, the letter she wrote to herself in 1992. The outside of the envelope said *"To: Cedar Rosenfield age 20! Private, Keep Out!"* Cedar opened it, reading it to me on her last birthday in 2001. We laughed together then as she stumbled through two pages of misspellings and observations written at half her age. But months later, reading it in her shadow, it made me ache for her, especially these few lines:

"I'm writing this for you to open when you're 20 years old. If you're reading this before 20, stop right now! I hope you have a good job dancing. If you do, what's it like? I am about to start dance lessons. What were they like? I hope you have a boyfriend. If you do, what's he like? From Cedar, age 10. P.S. Please write back."

"I don't know how a person without some kind of spiritual connection can live through losing their child." Ed and I strolled through our neighborhood during an already sweltering spring day in 2002.

A week earlier, I had had a Scientology counseling session that left me weak with relief. I hadn't believed it was possible to dampen this inferno of loss, but it had happened. "Not only does the bougainvillea look gorgeous again, but I can actually imagine a future." Ed squeezed my hand.

In late December of 2002 the phone rang. It was David calling us from Los Angeles.

"Hi Mom, Merry Christmas," he said cheerfully.

"Hi Sweetie. How was your holiday?"

"It was good." There was a pause.

"So what's happening?" I asked, alert to this sign of something important unsaid.

"Well... I'm moving to Clearwater!"

"Oh, David!" My eyes instantly filled with tears. And then "How soon will you be here?"

"It depends. I need to finish things up in L.A., probably a couple weeks at least."

It was closer to two months. He traveled east in February, at the same time we were traveling to a show in Ohio. We figured it out in advance and picked him up at a Greyhound Station somewhere in Tennessee.

"Hi Mom, Hi Dad." He was grinning, hauling a big duffle bag over one shoulder as he pushed open the glass door and hugged me with one arm.

He helped us set up the show, and we all stayed in the same hotel room. It was a snowy winter in Ohio that year— icicles dripped from the roof of the Knight's Inn, making it look a little like a Swedish Chalet. David brought out the Christmas present he had created for us in L.A. It was a drawing of him swing dancing with Cedar, in a frame he'd crafted himself from black-painted maple.

"It's beautiful," I told him. There were two gold circles of light above their heads, with musical notes surrounding and connecting them. I knew this was meant to represent the two of them as spirits.

"I love it, David." Ed's eyes were teary.

In Florida, David started his own business remodeling people's houses. The big Florida real estate boom was on and he had plenty of work.

Bob and Nancy's daughter Diana had moved back to Clearwater a year earlier, after graduating from college in West Virginia. She called one day, asking David if he'd help her with some Scientology volunteer work that weekend. His was just a familiar name from her past—she hadn't seen him since they both were toddlers.

David told her yes, but when he got off the phone he asked me, "Is she pretty?"

"She's beautiful," I said, and meant it. I'd seen Diana a few months earlier, when we'd had a sale in our living room of artwork donated by our friends for the Cedar Bennett Project, a non-profit we had started after Cedar died. Our first project was a documentary film about our daughter, cathartic for us and, we hoped, inspiring for young artists. For the benefit I'd set up two long tables of crafts in our living room and hung handcrafted clothing on borrowed stands and draped some over chairs.

"I'll take this scarf," Diana smiled at me with the whitest unbleached teeth I'd ever seen. She was slim, wore no makeup and had beautiful eyes.

"Thank you, Honey," I said and handed her the change.

Diana picked David up on Saturday morning and they were gone for several hours. When he walked in the door mid-afternoon I said, "Did you have fun?"

"Yes," he was smiling. I knew that look. David was smitten.

But Diana had recently broken up with her college sweetheart and was still savoring her singleness. "Just give her time," I encouraged David. "Get to know each other better."

David took Diana and her sister Katherine to Busch Gardens one weekend and the following one the two of them helped Ed and me tile our kitchen. Diana had a wide, easy laugh, I noticed, pleased.

"She'd be perfect in our family," I thought to myself, and then told Ed.

"Just cool it," Ed warned me with a sideways look.

But in a month they were holding hands and smooching. By June, David had moved into her house and a week later called us in our hotel room in Pittsburgh. He left a message for us to call him back that night. "It's important," he said.

"So what's up?" I asked, even though I knew what it had to be.

"I asked Diana to marry me, and she said yes," David told me, joy in his voice.

I screamed happily, surprising myself and making Ed jump. "That's wonderful! Have you set a date yet?"

"Yes. The end of July."

That was four weeks away. "Oh, Honey, how will our families come on such short notice?"

But of course they all did, traveling from New York, Kentucky and Rhode Island. Everyone waved colorful fans back and forth to keep the muggy July air in motion while David and Diana said their vows under the huge old oak in their front yard. They'd asked me to sing, so I played my dulcimer for the first time publicly since Cedar's memorial service. I'm sure my mother cried, but through her dark glasses it was hard to tell.

A little over a year later our granddaughter Ada was born, welcomed into the world in David and Diana's bedroom with a soft-voiced midwife steering them through. Nancy and I were there too, quietly encouraging Diana and handing the midwife warm compresses. David rubbed the small of Diana's back, the place where she felt the contractions most strongly.

Finally, we could see the baby's damp hair and in one grand push, the head was out. "The shoulder's stuck," the midwife said calmly, but she worked furiously to try and release her from the birth canal. The baby wasn't crying and her face had turned blue. "Come on, Sweetie, now PUSH!" the midwife coordinated Diana's efforts with her own, and in what seemed like minutes but must have been seconds, the baby emerged, quiet and still.

She was wrapped in a tiny white blanket and placed on her side, oxygen directed towards her nose and mouth from a portable canister. Nancy and I no longer clung to each other desperately, but hovered as our granddaughter at last turned pink and let out her first wail—a pure sound, like the beginning of everything.

Diana held her baby and wept with exhaustion, joy and relief. David kissed her forehead tenderly as she brought her child to the breast for the first time.

Afterward, the midwife asked Nancy and me if we'd like to dress our new granddaughter. Maybe it was all those years passed since either of us had our own wiggly newborn, but pinning a cotton diaper on that tiny rear end, then slipping a gown over her head took intense concentration from us both. She was eight and a half pounds of howling indignation, tiny arms and legs pumping furiously.

"Oh, my," Nancy said with a laugh.

Now Ada is an impish five-year-old who only occasionally lets her mother put her unruly mass of brown hair in neat pigtailed braids. All four grandparents have nicknames for this dark-eyed child that are definitely not interchangeable. For instance, to me she's Puddin' Cakes, but if I call her Granddaddy's pet name Muffin Chops, I get corrected. "No Grammy, call me Puddin Cakes," she says firmly.

In the car she tells her mom, "Play 'I Want to be a Country Girl Again,'" and sings along with Buffy St. Marie at the top of her lungs. You can't sing with her, it's a private concert and she has her rules. Her dad writes music, and sometimes at a performance she joins in with one of her own songs, adding strains of "Twinkle, Twinkle Little Star" to whatever David is playing at that moment.

David writes simple, lovely songs about his life. He calls his music "folk punk" and when he sings and plays his guitar, I can't take my eyes off his earnest face. Lucky for anyone listening, David sings so that you can actually hear every word.

One night in early summer he played at a club in Ybor city. The stage had a brick wall behind it and three lights shining straight down from the ceiling, which made the atmosphere sort of 1960-ish coffeehouse. David had a drummer that night—a plump, friendly youngster whose beat punctuated David's music in an interesting new way. "They sound good together," I shouted in Ed's ear, trying to gauge my volume so I wouldn't blow out his eardrum.

During a break I told David, "Maybe you should talk to the audience in between songs." From my own experience, a bar audience seems more interested in impressing each other than listening to live music. God knows it takes a lot to get their attention.

He smiled at me. "Okay, Mom, I'll try to remember."

I used to remind David and Cedar how powerful they were, capable of doing whatever they wanted and most importantly and dear to my heart, that they could make a living as artists. I love that David is playing music again.

When his concert was over, Ed and I looked for a snack before heading home. We found veggie tamales in a place billed as "Alaska Mex."

The young woman who took our order had a pierced nose and tattoos. She looked at me in a kindly way and I realized, momentarily startled and inexplicably embarrassed, that I look old now, like a hippie grandmother.

I was a little melancholy walking around Ybor City afterwards, because it was one of Cedar's hangouts where she'd go with her pals to dance rockabilly on the weekends.

We walked past The Italian Club, a gigantic turn of the century (not the most recent turn) brick building on East 7th Street. One time Cedar talked us into taking her to a dance there, before she got her driver's license.

The dance floor was upstairs, in a huge ballroom with decorative plaster molding and a hundred young people wearing their greased back hair, tattoos and poodle skirts jumping and jiving to 1950s swing. "The grease the guys use comes in different weights, just like car oil," she once told me, laughing.

After Ed and I dropped her off we walked around the Ybor City streets, feeling out of place at the dance, although Cedar wouldn't have cared a whit if we'd stayed. Oddly and wonderfully for us, she was never embarrassed by our presence.

"I still miss her so much." Ed put his arm around me as we walked through the now quiet streets.

The next day, I looked from my studio windows at the mango leaves fluttering in a pre-storm wind. My eyes stared comfortably, in a way that's only possible if you're not driving down the freeway or slicing tomatoes with a sharp knife.

I drifted back to twenty years in the past, to the fire that destroyed one of our favorite places to hike in southern California. After only one season, tender green plants peeked through the black ash. "Look Mommy, it's growing again!" Eight-year-old Cedar squatted above a shoot, fingering it gently.

There was a knock at the studio door, just a few feet above the bottom. I said "Who is it?" in my teasing Grammy voice.

"It's me!" I opened the door to Ada in her feathered-green play dress, Diana smiling behind her. "Do you have some carrot juice?" she handed me her stainless steel cup, permanently orange around the white sipping top. I grabbed her in my arms and nuzzled her soft neck while she shrieked with laughter.